USAF PLANS AND OPERATIONS

THE AIR CAMPAIGN AGAINST NORTH VIETNAM

1966

(U)

by

Jacob Van Staaveren

USAF Historical Division Liaison Office

January 1968

Published by Books Express Publishing
Copyright © Books Express, 2012
ISBN 978-1-78039-995-9

Books Express publications are available from all good retail and online booksellers. For publishing proposals and direct ordering please contact us at: info@books-express.com

FOREWORD

USAF Plans and Operations: The Air Campaign Against North Vietnam, 1966, is the seventh of a series of historical studies on the war in Southeast Asia prepared by the USAF Historical Division Liaison Office. The previous monographs covered plans, policies, and operations in the theater beginning in 1961.

The current history reviews the political background and top level discussions leading to the renewed bombing campaign in early 1966, the restrictions still imposed on air operations, and the positions taken on them by the military chiefs. It discusses the various studies and events which led to the President's decision to strike at North Vietnam's oil storage facilities and the results of those mid-year attacks. It also examines the increasing effectiveness of enemy air defenses and the continuing assessments of the air campaign under way at year's end.

MAX ROSENBERG
Chief
USAF Historical Division
  Liaison Office

NOTE

Listed below are the code names of certain air concepts, operations, programs, and aircraft cited in this study. The reader may find it helpful to refer to the list on occasion.

Barrel Roll — Initiated in December 1964, Barrel Roll missions were flown against troops, equipment and supplies provided by North Vietnam in support of the Communist-led Pathet Lao.

Combat Beaver — An air concept developed by the Air Staff in conjunction with the other services during September-November 1966. It was designed to support a proposed electronic and ground barrier system between North and South Vietnam.

Flaming Dart — The initial Navy and Air Force retaliatory air strikes against North Vietnam on 7-8 and 11 February 1965.

Gate Guard — An air program designed to slow North Vietnamese infiltration toward the demilitarized zone. It began on 1 May 1966 in the northern part of Laos and then shifted into route package area I in North Vietnam.

Iron Hand — Operations begun in August 1965 to locate and destroy Soviet-provided SA-2 missile sites in North Vietnam.

Rolling Thunder — The major air campaign begun on 2 March 1965 which inaugurated regularly scheduled air strikes against North Vietnam.

Steel Tiger — Initiated in April 1965, Steel Tiger strikes were made against infiltration routes south of the 17th parallel in Laos.

Tally-Ho — An air interdiction program started on 20 June 1966 in the southern part of North Vietnam, aimed at slowing the infiltration of North Vietnamese troops, equipment, and supplies through the demilitarized zone into South Vietnam.

Tiger Hound - Begun in December 1965, these strikes were aimed at infiltration targets in southern Laos. They featured for the first time in Laos the use of forward air controllers and airborne command and control for certain strikes.

Wild Weasel - USAF aircraft, largely F-100F's and F-105F's, specially equipped with electronic and other devices to neutralize or destroy Soviet-provided SA-2 sites in North Vietnam.

CONTENTS

FOREWORD

NOTE

I. OBJECTIVES OF THE AIR WAR AGAINST NORTH VIETNAM 1

    Background to Rolling Thunder 1
    The Air Force and JCS Urge Early Renewed Bombing 4
    Secretary McNamara's Views 7
    The Bombing Resumes and Further Air Planning 9

II. INCREASING THE AIR PRESSURE ON NORTH VIETNAM 14

    Air Operations and Analyses 14
    The Beginning of Rolling Thunder Program 50 18
    The Rolling Thunder Study of 6 April 22
    Air Operations in May: Beginning of Gate Guard 25
    Highlights of June Operations 27

III. THE POL STRIKES AND NEW ROLLING THUNDER PROGRAM 51 . . . 29

    Background of the POL Air Strikes 29
    The Strikes of 29 June 31
    The Mid-1966 Assessment 33
    The Beginning of Rolling Thunder Program 51 35
    The Tally-Ho Air Campaign 38

IV. ANALYSES OF THE AIR CAMPAIGN 43

    Operational Studies 43
    The Effectiveness of Air Power 45
    Studies on Aircraft Attrition 49
    The Hise Report 52
    Secretary McNamara's Proposal to Reduce Aircraft Attrition . . . 56

V. THE AIR WAR AT YEAR'S END 58

    Approval of Rolling Thunder Program 52 59
    The Furor over Air Strikes "on Hanoi" 60
    Other Air Operations in November and December 62
    Assessment of Enemy Air Defenses 63
    Assessments of the Air War Against North Vietnam 67

NOTES 72

APPENDICES 82

    Appendix 1 - U.S. and VNAF Attack Sorties in Southeast Asia 82
    Appendix 2 - B-52 Sorties in Southeast Asia 82
    Appendix 3 - U.S. and VNAF Attack Sorties in North Vietnam 83
    Appendix 4 - U.S. Aircraft Losses in Southeast Asia 84
    Appendix 5 - USAF Combat Attrition in North Vietnam 85
    Appendix 6 - U.S. Aircraft Losses to SA-2's 85
    Appendix 7 - SA-2 Sites in North Vietnam 86
    Appendix 8 - Light and Medium Antiaircraft Artillery Guns
                  in North Vietnam. 86
    Appendix 9 - U.S. Aircraft Losses in Aerial Combat 87
    Appendix 10 - North Vietnamese Aircraft Losses in Aerial Combat 87

GLOSSARY 88

MAP 3
    Route Package Areas, North Vietnam 3

CHART 64
    Chronology of the Growth of North Vietnam's Air Defenses 64

I. OBJECTIVES OF THE AIR WAR AGAINST NORTH VIETNAM

From its inception, the "out-of-country" air campaign in Southeast Asia, that is, against targets in North Vietnam and Laos, was limited in scope and objective. The first air strikes against North Vietnam were conducted on 5 August 1964 by Navy aircraft in retaliation for Communist attacks on U.S. ships in the Gulf of Tonkin. The next ones occurred on 7-8 and 11 February 1965 when USAF and Navy aircraft flew "Flaming Dart" I and II missions in retaliation for Viet Cong assaults on U.S. military bases in South Vietnam. These were followed by an air program against selected North Vietnamese targets in order to exert, slowly and progressively, more military pressure on the Hanoi regime. Designated "Rolling Thunder," it began on 2 March 1965. As explained by Secretary of Defense Robert S. McNamara, the air attacks had three main purposes: raise South Vietnamese morale, reduce the infiltration of men and supplies to South Vietnam and increase its cost, and force the Communists at some point to the negotiating table.*

Background to Rolling Thunder

The Rolling Thunder program was basically a USAF-Navy air effort but included occasional token sorties by the Vietnamese Air Force (VNAF). Adm. U.S. Grant Sharp, Commander-in-Chief, Pacific (CINCPAC), Honolulu, exercised operational control through the commanders of the Pacific Air Forces (PACAF), the Seventh Fleet, and the Military Assistance, Command, Vietnam (MACV). Coordination control was assigned to the PACAF commander with the tacit understanding that it would be further delegated to Maj. Gen. Joseph H. Moore, Jr.,

---

* For highlights of the air war against North Vietnam and Laos prior to 1966, see Jacob Van Staaveren, <u>USAF Plans and Policies in South Vietnam and Laos,</u> (AFCHO, 1964), and <u>USAF Plans and Operations in Southeast Asia,</u> (AFCHO, 1965).

commander of the 2d Air Division (predecessor of the Seventh Air Force) in South Vietnam. Both the Air Staff and the PACAF commander considered this arrangement inefficient, believing that air assets in Southeast Asia, with few exceptions, should be under the control of a single Air Force commander.[1]

With the air program carefully circumscribed, the North Vietnamese initially enjoyed extensive sanctuaries. These included the Hanoi-Haiphong area and the northeastern and northwestern portions of the country closest to China. Targets were selected by the Joint Chiefs of Staff (JCS) after considering the recommendations of Admiral Sharp and the MACV commander, Gen. William C. Westmoreland, the decisions being based on intelligence from the war theater and in Washington. The Secretary of Defense reviewed the recommendations and then submitted them to the President for final approval. Special targeting committees performed this vital task.[2]

Rolling Thunder at first was characterized by individually approved air strikes but, as the campaign progressed, the high authorities approved one- and two-week target "packages" in advance and also gradually expanded the bombing area. In August 1965 they narrowed North Vietnam's sanctuaries to a 30-nautical mile radius of Hanoi, a 10-nautical mile radius of Haiphong, a 25-nautical mile "buffer" near the Chinese border extending from the coast to longitude 106^c E. and a 30-nautical mile buffer from longitude 106^c E. westward to the Laos border. By early September armed reconnaissance sorties had reached a rate of about 600 per week and did not rise above this figure during the remainder of the year. There was a reduction in the number of fixed targets that could be hit[*] and no extension of the bombing area. Poor weather contributed to the static sortie rate after September.[3]

---

[*] However, the list of 220 fixed targets as of 20 September was not reduced.

ROUTE PACKAGE AREAS
NORTH VIETNAM
22 Apr 66

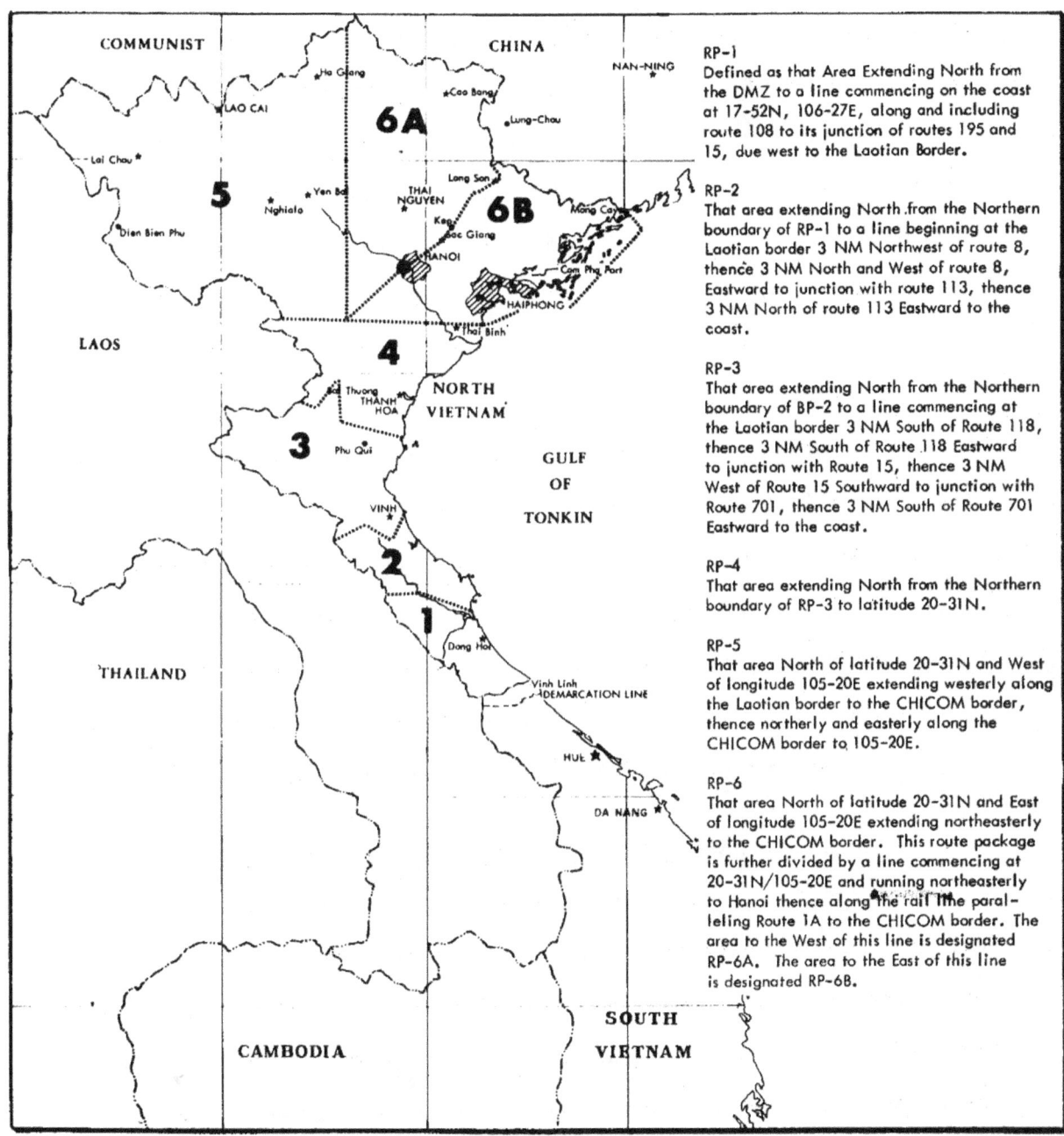

RP-1
Defined as that Area Extending North from the DMZ to a line commencing on the coast at 17-52N, 106-27E, along and including route 108 to its junction of routes 195 and 15, due west to the Laotian Border.

RP-2
That area extending North from the Northern boundary of RP-1 to a line beginning at the Laotian border 3 NM Northwest of route 8, thence 3 NM North and West of route 8, Eastward to junction with route 113, thence 3 NM North of route 113 Eastward to the coast.

RP-3
That area extending North from the Northern boundary of BP-2 to a line commencing at the Laotian border 3 NM South of Route 118, thence 3 NM South of Route 118 Eastward to junction with Route 15, thence 3 NM West of Route 15 Southward to junction with Route 701, thence 3 NM South of Route 701 Eastward to the coast.

RP-4
That area extending North from the Northern boundary of RP-3 to latitude 20-31N.

RP-5
That area North of latitude 20-31N and West of longitude 105-20E extending westerly along the Laotian border to the CHICOM border, thence northerly and easterly along the CHICOM border to 105-20E.

RP-6
That area North of latitude 20-31N and East of longitude 105-20E extending northeasterly to the CHICOM border. This route package is further divided by a line commencing at 20-31N/105-20E and running northeasterly to Hanoi thence along the rail line paralleling Route 1A to the CHICOM border. The area to the West of this line is designated RP-6A. The area to the East of this line is designated RP-6B.

Source: USAF Mgt Summary, 22 Apr 66

In November 1965 there was an important change in bombing procedure when Admiral Sharp, at the Navy's request, divided North Vietnam into six principal "route packages." Each included lines of communication (LOC's) and other targets suitable for armed reconnaissance strikes and were to be assigned to the Air Force or Navy for a two-week period, the duration of specific Rolling Thunder programs at that time. (Service air strikes against fixed JCS-numbered targets were excepted and took precedence over armed reconnaissance operations.) Starting 10 December, the Air Force began armed reconnaissance flights in route packages II, IV, and V, and the Navy in route packages I and III.* General Moore, commander of the 2d Air Division, was dissatisfied with this split system of air responsibility. He felt it continued to forfeit the advantages of centralized air control under which the complementing capabilities of Air Force and Navy aircraft could be better coordinated.[4]

(U) On 24 December 1965 the Americans began a two-day Christmas bombing pause in the air campaign against the North which eventually grew into a 37-day moratorium as the U.S. government made a major effort to find a basis for negotiating an end to the war. The limited bombing of targets in Laos and the air and ground war in South Vietnam continued, however.[5]

The Air Force and JCS Urge Early Renewed Bombing

Both the Air Staff and the USAF Chief of Staff, Gen. John P. McConnell, were deeply troubled by the bombing moratorium. Testifying before Senate committees early in January 1966, General McConnell observed that it enabled Hanoi to move men, supplies, and equipment around the clock and to restore its lines of communication. A delay in resuming attacks could

---
* With variations, the rotation policy continued until April 1966. See p 21.

prove costly in lives. Concerned about the relative ineffectiveness of the 1965 bombing effort, he favored removing political restraints on the use of air power to allow heavier strikes before a major U.S. and allied force buildup, then under consideration by the administration, was approved. He thought that the military effort against North Vietnam should have a priority equal to that given by the administration to the war in the South.[6]

Other service chiefs supported General McConnell's recommendations to resume and intensify the bombing of the North. On 8 January 1966 they informed Secretary McNamara that the bombing pause was greatly weakening the U.S. negotiating "leverage" and proving advantageous to Hanoi, permitting it to reconstitute its forces and continue infiltration through Laos into South Vietnam. They recommended renewed bombing 48 hours after a Soviet delegation, then in Hanoi, returned to Moscow. Concerned about a possible Communist misinterpretation of U.S. resolve, the Joint Chiefs wanted to insure that any peace negotiations were pursued from a position of strength.[7]

After a Central Intelligence Agency (CIA) and Defense Intelligence Agency (DIA) analysis confirmed that the 1965 bombings had failed to halt the resupply of Communist forces, the JCS prepared another recommendation for Secretary McNamara. On 18 January it urged, again in accordance with General McConnell's view, that the bombing moratorium end with a "sharp blow" followed by expanded air operations throughout the North. It suggested reducing the "sanctuary" areas to a 10-nautical-mile radius of Hanoi and Phuc Yen airfield, a 4-nautical mile radius of Haiphong, and a 20-nautical-mile "buffer" zone in the northeast and northwest areas near the Chinese border. The JCS also called for closing the major seaports (by mining) and removing other political restraints against striking important targets.[8]

On 25 January, in answer to a query from Secretary McNamara, the JCS proposed three alternate ways to resume the bombing. One would use all Thai-based USAF aircraft and planes from three Navy carriers, flying 450 sorties per day for 72 hours, hitting all land and water targets (vehicles, ferries, pontoon bridges, etc.) outside of the sanctuary areas. The second would use the same aircraft flying armed reconnaissance against all LOC and petroleum, oil, and lubricants (POL) targets for 24 to 72 hours with follow-on attacks in accordance with the first alternative. The third called for 600 armed reconnaissance sorties per week in southern North Vietnam with the tempo being increased until the target program recommended on 18 January was reached.[9]

In addition to their proposals to renew the bombing, the Joint Chiefs examined ways to improve air activity. They sent Admiral Sharp guidance on making more effective air strikes against watercraft on inland waterways in the North. Until the bombing halt, more watercraft had been observed as air attacks on the road and rail network had forced the North Vietnamese to rely increasingly on water transportation. The Joint Chiefs concluded that better air-delivered mines should be developed and asked the Chief of Naval Operations (CNO) to give special attention to this matter.[10]

The JCS also examined the problem of closing down the 124-mile rail link between Hanoi and Lao Cai. This and the Hanoi Dong Dang line were the two principal rail arteries to the Chinese border. Secretary McNamara had expressed surprise that the Hanoi-Lao Cai segment was still in service despite repeated air strikes by USAF aircraft before the bombing pause. On 22 January, the JCS chairman, Gen. Earle G. Wheeler responded that there were two reasons why it remained open: frequent aborts because of weather during

December 1965 -- amounting to 37 percent of the planned sorties that month -- and the arrival of Chinese railway engineering personnel that substantially augmented the North Vietnamese repair capability. To keep the line closed, said General Wheeler, would require the destruction of three bridges, at least 100 armed reconnaissance sorties per week, and the use of reliable, long-delay bomb fuzes and seismic fuze antirailroad mines, both still under development.[11]

Secretary McNamara's Views

(U) The administration moved cautiously toward a decision on whether to renew the bombing of the North. On 19 January Secretary McNamara informed the Joint Chiefs that their views on this matter were under constant study by the State Department. On the 26th, in a summation of the 1965 Rolling Thunder program, the Defense Secretary told a House subcommittee:[12]

> It was clearly recognized that this pressure, by itself, would not ever be sufficient to cause North Vietnam to move toward negotiation unless it were accompanied by military action in South Vietnam that proved to the North that they could not win there. These were our objectives then; they are our objectives now. A corollary of these objectives is the avoidance of unnecessary military risk. We, therefore, have directed the bombing against the military targets, primarily routes of infiltration.
>
> We have not bombed Hanoi, we have not bombed Haiphong. We have not bombed certain petroleum supplies which are important. We have not mined the Haiphong port. We have gradually evolved from last February to mid-December, a target system that included all of North Vietnam except certain specified locations.
>
> The targets were very carefully chosen and the rate at which the bombing program grew was very carefully controlled, all for the purpose of trying to achieve our limited objective without widening the conflict.

(U) It was also Secretary McNamara's "strong personal opinion" that the war in South Vietnam could not be won solely by bombing the North and that the northern air campaign should be essentially a "supplement" to military action in the South.[13]

Although the air war was carefully limited, the Defense Secretary informed the President that it had already achieved the objective of raising the cost of infiltration. Air attacks had reduced the amount of enemy supplies reaching the South, carried mostly by trucks over greatly improved routes, from about 400 to 200 tons per day. Moreover, they had diverted 50,000 to 100,000 personnel* to air defense and repair work, hampered the mobility of the populace, forced decentralization of government activities thus creating more inefficiency and political risk, and reduced North Vietnam's activities in Laos.

For 1966, Secretary McNamara thought that the bombing "at a minimum" should include 4,000 attack sorties per month consisting of day and night armed reconnaissance against rail and road targets and POL storage sites except in cities and the buffer zone near the Chinese border. He proposed more intense bombing of targets in Laos, along the Bassac and Mekong rivers running into South Vietnam from Cambodia, and better surveillance of the sea approaches. In the South there should be more harassment of enemy LOC's and destruction of his bases.

Recognizing that estimates of enemy needs and capabilities and the results of air action "could be wrong by a factor of two either way," the Secretary advised the President that unless studies under way indicated otherwise, heavier bombing probably would not put a tight ceiling on the enemy's activities in South Vietnam. However, he thought it would reduce the flow of Communist supplies and limit the enemy's flexibility to undertake frequent offensive action or to defend himself adequately against U.S., allied,

---

* Estimates on the size of air defense and repair crews varied widely during 1966. See pp 34, 47, and 69.

and South Vietnamese troops. Mr. McNamara suggested two possible by-products of the bombing effort: it should help to condition Hanoi toward negotiation and an acceptable end to the war and it would maintain the morale of the South Vietnamese armed forces. The defense chief also outlined for the President the 1966 military objectives for South Vietnam.*[14]

The Bombing Resumes and Further Air Planning

(U) Having received no acceptable response from Hanoi to his peace overtures, President Johnson on 31 January ordered resumption of the bombing of North Vietnam. It began the same day. "Our air strikes . . . from the beginning," the President announced, "have been aimed at military targets and controlled with great care. Those who direct and supply the aggression have no claim to immunity from military reply." Other officials told newsmen that the United States would continue to limit bombing of the North but intensify other aspects of the war, including more use of B-52 bombers and ground artillery in South Vietnam.[15]

As anticipated, the bombing moratorium had in fact benefited the North Vietnamese. USAF reconnaissance revealed that supplies had moved by truck and rail 24 hours per day and that repairs and new construction on the road and rail net likewise had proceeded on a "round-the-clock" basis. General McConnell believed that the moratorium had permitted the North to

---

* The objectives were formalized during a meeting between President Johnson, and South Vietnamese Prime Minister, Nguyen Cao Ky at Honolulu from 6 to 8 February. They agreed to try to: (1) raise the casualty rate of Viet Cong-North Vietnamese forces to a level equal to their capability to put new men in the field; (2) increase the areas denied to the Communists from 10 to 20 percent to 40 to 50 percent; (3) increase the population in secure areas from 50 to 60 percent; (4) pacify four high-priority areas containing the following population: Da Nang, 387,000; Qui Nhon, 650,000; Hoa Hao, 800,000, and Saigon, 3,500,000; (5) increase from 30 to 50 percent the roads and rail lines open for use; and (6) insure the defense of all military bases, political and population centers, and food-producing areas under the control of the Saigon government.

strengthen its antiaircraft defenses, including expansion of its SA-2 system from about 50 to 60 sites. Admiral Sharp reported the enemy had deployed about 40 more air defense positions in the northwest rail line area and 26 more guns to protect routes south of Vinh.[16]

When the aerial attacks resumed as Rolling Thunder program 48, allied air strength in South Vietnam and Thailand consisted of about 689 U.S. and 125 Vietnamese Air Force tactical combat aircraft.* More would arrive in subsequent months. The limitations placed on the renewed bombing effort disappointed the Joint Chiefs, especially since none of their recommendations had been accepted. In fact, the program was more restrictive than before the bombing pause. Armed reconnaissance during February was limited to 300 sorties per day and almost solely to the four route package areas south of Hanoi. Only one JCS target, Dien Bien Phu airfield, was hit several times. Poor weather forced the cancellation of many strikes and others were diverted to targets in Laos. A Pacific Command (PACOM) assessment indicated that the renewed air effort was producing few important results as compared to those attained during 1965 against trucks, railroad rolling stock, and watercraft.[17]

Meanwhile, the bombing policy remained under intensive review. At the request of Secretary McNamara, General Wheeler on 1 February asked the service chiefs to establish a joint study group which would examine again the Rolling Thunder program and produce data that could serve as a basis for future JCS recommendations. They quickly organized the group under the leadership of Brig. Gen. Jammie M. Philpott, Director of Intelligence,

---

* The number of U.S. tactical combat aircraft by service were: Air Force, 355; Navy (three carriers), 209; and Marine Corps, 125. In addition the Air Force had 30 B-52's in Guam. (North Vietnam possessed about 75 MIG's.)

Strategic Air Command (SAC). Its report was not issued until April.[*][18]

On 8 February, following a three-week conference of service officials in Honolulu to plan U.S. and allied air and ground deployments, through fiscal year 1968, Admiral Sharp and his staff briefed Secretary McNamara on the results of their deliberations. They proposed a program of stepped up air attacks in the North and in Laos with the immediate goal of destroying Communist resources contributing to the aggression, and of harassing, disrupting, and impeding the movement of men and materiel. Admiral Sharp advocated 7,100 combat sorties per month for the North and 3,000 per month for the South.[19]

Secretary McNamara did not immediately respond to these sortie proposals. However, he approved, with certain modifications, CINCPAC's recommended schedule for additional air and ground forces. These deployments promised to strain severely the resources of the services, especially those of the Air Force and the Army. Concerned about their impact on the Air Force's "roles and missions," force structure, overall posture, and research and development needs, Lt. Gen. H.T. Wheless, Assistant Vice Chief of Staff on 18 February directed Headquarters USAF's Operations Analysis Office to undertake a "vigorous" analysis and asked all Air Staff offices to support the effort. Its major purpose was to develop a more comprehensive data base on the use of air power in Southeast Asia.[20]

Because of the decision to deploy more forces and the likelihood of stepped up air and ground operations, General McConnell decided a number of organizational changes were necessary. He directed the Air Staff to replace the 2nd Air Division with a numbered Air Force, upgrade the

---
[*] See p 22.

commander of the Thirteenth Air Force in the Philippines to three-star rank, and formalize USAF-Army airlift arrangements in the theater.* [21]

With the air campaign continuing at a low tempo, the JCS, with Air Staff support, reaffirmed its prior recommendation to Secretary McNamara for accelerated air operations against the North and to strike all targets still under administration wraps. If this could not be approved, the JCS urged extending operations at least to the previously authorized areas. The Joint Chiefs warned that if more remunerative targets could not be hit to compensate for the handicaps imposed by operational restraints, more air sorties should be flown elsewhere. They also raised their estimated sortie requirement for the northern campaign from 7,100 to 7,400 per month, citing Admiral Sharp's newly acquired intelligence which confirmed additional enemy deployments of SA-2 missiles and possible Chinese antiaircraft artillery units in the northeast region.[22]

Secretary McNamara informed the JCS that the political atmosphere was not favorable for implementing these recommendations. Some Air Staff members attributed the administration's cautiousness to the Senate Foreign Relations Committee hearings on the war, which began 4 February under the chairmanship of Senator J. William Fulbright. In addition, the Defense Secretary was known to believe that there were limitations to what air power could do in the type of war being waged in Southeast Asia. Mr. McNamara thought that even the obliteration of North Vietnam would not completely end that country's support of enemy operations in the South since most of the arms and ammunition came from other Communist nations. He firmly believed

---

* See Van Staaveren, 1966, p 40.

that the war would have to be won on the ground in South Vietnam.[23]

(U) Secretary of the Air Force Harold Brown echoed this administration position position, asserting publicly on 25 February that the destruction of the North's remaining industrial capacity would neither prevent the resupply of equipment and troops in the South nor end hostilities. He also said:[24]

> . . . should it appear that we were trying to destroy North Vietnam, the prospect of escalation by the other side would increase, and with it would increase the possibility of heavier U.S. casualties and an even harder and longer war . . . .
>
> . . . our objective is not to destroy North Vietnam. It is to stop aggression against South Vietnam at the lowest feasible cost in lives and property. We should take the course that is most likely to bring a satisfactory outcome . . . at a comparately low risk and low cost to ourselves. Our course is to apply increasing pressure in South Vietnam both by ground and supporting air attacks; to make it clear to the North Vietnamese and Viet Cong forces . . . that life is going to get more difficult for them . . . that war is expensive and dangerous.

(U) Thus, for the time being, the JCS-recommended program for an accelerated air campaign against North Vietnam had no chance of receiving administration approval.

II. INCREASING THE AIR PRESSURE ON NORTH VIETNAM

On 1 March the JCS generally endorsed Admiral Sharp's "Case I"* air, ground, and naval deployment program leading to stepped-up operations against the Communists in North and South Vietnam and Laos. It also recommended again that the war be fought in accordance with the Concept for Vietnam paper which it had approved on 27 August 1965 and later amended. This paper called for air strikes against the North's war-supporting industries in the Hanoi-Haiphong area, aerial mining of the ports, additional interdiction of inland and coastal waterways, and special air and ground operations in Laos -- all recommended many times in various ways. But administration authorities continued to favor a more modest air effort against the Hanoi regime.[1]

Air Operations and Analyses

The new Rolling Thunder program -- number 49 -- was ushered in on 1 March. It was still limited to armed reconnaissance of the North but the administration had broadened the authorized attack area to include coastal regions and had eased restrictions to permit the use of air power up to the level existing when bombing ceased on 24 December 1965. The Air Force and Navy were allocated a total of 5,100 armed reconnaissance sorties (and 3,000 for Laos), with the number to be flown by each contingent on weather and other operational factors. Poor weather, however, limited their sorties to 4,491 during the month. The Air Force concentrated its efforts against targets in route packages I, III, and VIA, the Navy in route

---

* Case I called for deployment of a total of 413,557 U.S. personnel in South Vietnam by the end of calendar year 1966.

packages II and IV and against coastal targets in route package I through IV. The VNAF flew token sorties in route package I under the protection of U.S. Marine Corps electronic and escort aircraft. On 10 March the JCS again pressed for its proposed accelerated air program with early attacks on POL sites, the main rail system running from China, and the mining of deep water ports. Again the recommendation was not acted upon.[2]

Meanwhile, the North's air defense system began to pose a greater threat to USAF and Navy operations. On 3 March photo reconnaissance aircraft discovered about 25 MIG-21 fuselage crates at Phuc Yen airfield near Hanoi. USAF "Big Eye" EC-121D aircraft also detected airborne MIG's about 55 times during March, although there were no engagements. Admiral Sharp directed the PACAF and Seventh Fleet commanders to prepare for counter-air operations and the SAC commander to submit a plan for a B-52 strike, if necessary, against Phuc Yen and Kep airfields.* He asked for additional electronically equipped USAF EB-66 aircraft to reduce the effectiveness of the SA-2 missiles and the antiaircraft guns. "Jamming" was thought to have already reduced the usefulness of enemy air defenses.[3]

Aircraft losses to enemy ground fire continued to cause much concern. A Joint Staff study of the problem during March showed that 199 American aircraft had been lost over North Vietnam since the bombings began on 7 February 1965, sixteen of them by SA-2 missiles.

---
* Gen Curtis E. LeMay, former CSAF, first recommended striking the North's airfields on 10 August 1964 and the JCS sent its first recommendation to do so on 14 November 1964. By 1 March 1966 the JCS had made a total of 11 such recommendations but the administration had approved strikes on only three small airfields at Vinh, Dong Hoi, and Dien Bien Phu in May 1965, June 1965, and February 1966 respectively.

The aircraft loss rate was six times higher in the northeast, the most heavily defended area, than in the rest of North Vietnam. Headquarters USAF estimated the North's antiaircraft strength at 2,525 guns.*[4]

To improve its analysis of aircraft losses and other operational data, the Air Staff on 26 March established an ad hoc study group in the Directorate of Operations. In the same month the Chief of Operations Analysis, in response to General Wheless' directive of 17 February, completed an initial study on the effectiveness of air interdiction in Southeast Asia. It summarized the enemy's supply requirements, his capability to transport supplies by land or sea, and the extent air strikes had hampered such activities. One conclusion was that air attacks had not yet decreased the movement of men and supplies from the North through Laos to South Vietnam. They had, however, inflicted about $15 to $16 million direct and $8 million indirect damage on the North's economy and forced Hanoi to recruit 30,000 more personnel, in addition to local forces, to perform repair work. An analysis of one route from Vinh to Muang Phine suggested that air attacks had caused the Communists to increase their truck inventory by one-third and their transport time by two-thirds.[5]

Another Operations Analysis interdiction study listed enemy targets destroyed or damaged in North Vietnam and Laos through March 1966 as follows:

---

* Estimates of North Vietnam's antiaircraft gun inventory varied considerably during 1966. See Admiral Sharp's estimate of July, p 34, the Seventh Air Force's estimate for January and December 1966, p 64, and a final estimate, app 8.

	North Vietnam			Laos		
	Des	Dam	Total	Des	Dam	Total
Transportation Vehicles	1,537	2,500	4,307	515	485	1,000
LOC Network *	546	4,381	4,927	398	4,886	5,284
Counter-Air +	134	189	323	145	67	145
All Other ++	3,681	4,196	7,877	2,783	1,259	3,997
Total	5,898	11,266	17,164	3,841	6,697	10,426

Concerning the Communist effort to fill craters and repair roads damaged by air attacks, there were indications that only one man-day of direct productive effort per attack sortie was needed to perform this task. "At this rate," the Operations Analysis study observed, "a few hundred sorties per day would only make enough work for a few hundred men."

As for Communist supplies, the study estimated that in 1965 they averaged 51 tons per day across the North Vietnamese-Laos border and 16 tons per day across the Laos-South Vietnamese border. For 1966 (through March), the figures were 70 and 35 tons respectively. The Laos panhandle infiltration routes in themselves appeared to be capable, despite air attacks, of supporting the current low-level combat by Viet Cong and North Vietnamese forces. To support a higher combat level, for example, one day in seven, the Communists would have to use other supply channels or dip into South Vietnamese stockpiles, either of which would complicate their distribution problems.[6]

---

* Included bridges, road cuts, rail cuts, ferry ships.

+ Included aircraft, runways, antiaircraft sites, SA-2 sites, and radar sites.

++ Included buildings, POL tanks, power plants, locks and dams.

The Beginning of Rolling Thunder Program 50

Concurrently, there was planning for the next Rolling Thunder program. In meetings with General Wheeler on 21 and 23 March, Secretary McNamara set forth certain guidelines for stepping up air strikes in the northeast and hitting additional JCS targets. The Joint Chiefs quickly responded by proposing Rolling Thunder program 50. It called for launching 900 attack sorties against major lines of communication and striking nine POL storage areas, six bridges, one iron and steel plant, one early warning and ground control intercept (EW/GCI) site, and one cement plant, the latter in Haiphong. Admiral Sharp planned to conduct this program within an allocation of 8,100 sorties (5,100 for North Vietnam, 3,000 for Laos).[7]

Administration authorities approved this program, which began on 1 April. For the first time in 1966 armed reconnaissance was authorized over the far northeast and four new JCS targets (all rail and highway bridges) were cleared for interdiction. However, some time before program 50 ended on 9 July, permission to strike the other JCS-recommended targets was withdrawn. Dissatisfied with the restrictions, General McConnell and the Marine Corps chief jointly advised the JCS that "sound military judgment" dictated that all the targets be hit immediately. Higher administration officials withheld consent, however, principally because of the unstable South Vietnamese political situation which developed after the ruling junta's ouster on 10 March of Lt. Gen. Nguyen Chanh Thi, the I Corps commander.[8]

Poor weather in April again limited the number of attack sorties flown against the North and delayed until 5 May the completion of strikes against the four authorized JCS targets. Other air operations included armed reconnaissance against roads, rail lines, watercraft and similar LOC targets. April also saw several important developments: establishment of the Seventh Air Force, the first B-52 strike in North Vietnam, a marked step-up in Hanoi's air defense effort that resulted in a U.S. downing of the first MIG-21, a change in the command and control of route package I, and the beginning of a study on increasing air pressure to offset civil disturbances in South Vietnam.[9]

The establishment of the Seventh Air Force, effective 8 April, followed General McConnell's successful efforts to raise the stature of the major USAF operational command in the theater. General Moore continued to serve as its chief with no change in his relationship with other commanders. Also, in accordance with General McConnell's wishes, the commander of the Thirteenth Air Force in the Philippines was raised to three-star rank on 1 July.[10]

SAC made the first B-52 strike against the North on 12 April when 30 bombers dropped 7,000 tons of 750- and 1,000-pound bombs on a road segment of Mugia Pass near the Laotian border. It was believed to be the single greatest air attack on a target since World War II. Initial reports indicated that "route 15" had been "definitely closed" by a landslide as had been hoped; however, 26 1/2 hours later reconnaissance photos showed all the craters filled in and the road appeared serviceable, attesting to the quick repair capability of the North Vietnamese. A second strike by 15 B-52's on 26 April on a road segment six kilometers north of Mugia blocked the road for only 18 hours. The apparent inability of the B-52's to close down the road -- expressed by the Secretary of State and other officials -- and a Seventh Air Force report of an SA-2 site near Mugia, prompted Admiral Sharp on 30 April to recommend to the JCS no further attacks on the pass.

In fact, the bombers were not again used near North Vietnam until 30 July.*[11]

Towards the end of April Hanoi stepped up its air defense activity, dispatching 29 to 31 MIG's against USAF and Navy aircraft. In nine separate engagements in five days, six MIG's were destroyed, all by USAF F-4C's which suffered no losses. The first MIG-21 was downed on 26 April by two F-4C's. Antiaircraft fire continued to account for most American aircraft combat losses with 31 downed (14 USAF, 17 Navy), while two -- an F-102 and a Navy A-1H -- were struck by SA-2 missiles.[12]

Meanwhile, a change in command and control of air operations in route package I followed a meeting on 28 March between Admiral Sharp and the JCS. The PACOM commander recommended that General Westmoreland's request for partial operational control of this area be approved and that the sector be accorded the same priority as for South Vietnam and Laotian "Tiger Hound" air operations. General Westmoreland urgently desired more air power to hit enemy approaches to the battlefield area near the Demilitarized Zone (DMZ) for which he was responsible. Admiral Sharp thought that 3,500 sorties a month was warranted alone for route package I.[13]

USAF commanders and the Air Staff objected to the proposed change, feeling that MACV's command authority should be limited to South Vietnam. They believed that the PACAF commander should remain the sole coordinating authority for the Rolling Thunder program. Nevertheless, Secretary McNamara approved the change on 14 April and the JCS endorsed it on the 20th. To allay any doubts where he thought the war's emphasis should be, the defense chief said that air operations north of route package I could be carried out only if they did not penalize air operations in the

---

* See p 40.

"extended battlefield," that is, in South Vietnam, the Tiger Hound area of Laos, and route package area I. Under this change Admiral Sharp still retained partial operational control of route package I. General Westmoreland's authority was limited to armed photo reconnaissance and intelligence analysis of Rolling Thunder and "Iron Hand" operations. Simultaneously, the Air Force-Navy rotational bombing procedure in other route packages, in effect since late 1966, also ended.* 14

The civil disturbances and reduced U.S. and allied military activity in both South and North Vietnam that followed General Thi's dismissal+ prompted the Joint Staff on 14 April to recommend a step-up in the attacks in accordance with the JCS proposals of 18 January. It thought this might help arrest the deteriorating situation. A special Joint Staff study of the problem also examined the possibility that a government coming to power in Saigon might wish to end the war and ask U.S. and allied forces to leave. 15

The Air Staff generally supported the Joint Staff's recommendation for an intensified air offensive against the North and withdrawal of U.S. forces if a local fait accompli left the United States and its allies no choice. But the Army's Chief of Staff doubted that heavier air strikes could resolve the political situation in South Vietnam. Observing that Admiral Sharp already possessed authority to execute some of the recommended strikes, he opposed sending the Joint Staff's study to Secretary McNamara on the grounds that if U.S. strategy was to be reevaluated it should be by separate action. General McConnell suggested, and the JCS agreed, to consider alternate ways of withdrawing part or all of the U.S.

---

* See p 4.

+ See p 18.

forces from South Vietnam should this be necessary. Reviews were begun but in subsequent weeks, after political stability was gradually restored, the need to consider withdrawal action lessened and no final decisions were taken.[16]

The Rolling Thunder Study of 6 April

(U) April also witnessed the completion of the special joint report on the Rolling Thunder program requested by Secretary McNamara in February. Prepared under the direction of General Philpott,* it was based on all data available in Washington plus information collected by staff members who visited PACOM, MACV, the 2d Air Division, and the Seventh Fleet.

Completed on 6 April, the Philpott report reviewed the results of one year of Rolling Thunder operations (2 March 1965-2 March 1966). During this period U.S. and VNAF aircraft had flown about 45,000 combat and 20,000 combat support sorties, damaging or destroying 6,100 "fixed" targets (bridges, ferry facilities, military barracks, supply depots, etc.), and 3,400 "mobile" targets (trucks, railroad rolling stock, and watercraft). American combat losses totaled about 185 aircraft.

The report touched briefly on Laos where the air effort consisted primarily of armed reconnaissance in two principal areas designated as "Barrel Roll" and "Steel Tiger." It noted that the effectiveness of USAF strikes in Laos was limited because of small fixed targets, high jungle growth, and mountainous terrain that hampered target location and identification. Also, important targets were normally transitory and had to be confirmed carefully before they could be attacked. The operations in North Vietnam and Laos, said the report:

---
* See pp 10-11.

. . . have achieved a degree of success within the parameters of imposed restrictions. However, the restricted scope of operations, the restraints and piecemealing effort, have degraded program effectiveness to a level well below the optimum. Because of this, the enemy has received war-supporting materiel from external sources, through routes of ingress, which for the most part have been immune from attack, and has dispersed and stored this materiel in politically assured sanctuaries. . . . Although air operations caused significant disruption prior to the standdown, there has been an increase in the North Vietnamese logistic infiltration program, indicating a much greater requirement for supplies in South Vietnam. . . .

Of a total of 236 "JCS numbered" targets in North Vietnam, 134 had been struck, including 42 bridges. Among the 102 untouched targets, 90 were in the northeast area and, of these, 70 were in the sanctuary zones of Hanoi, Haiphong, and the "buffer" territory near China. Elsewhere in the North 86 percent of the JCS targets had been hit. The report further asserted:

> The less than optimum air campaign, and the uninterrupted receipt of supplies from Russia, China, satellite countries, and certain elements of the free world have undoubtedly contributed to Hanoi's belief in ultimate victory. Therefore . . . the Study Group considers it essential that the air campaign be redirected against specific target systems, critical to the capability and important to the will of North Vietnam to continue aggression and support insurgency.

It consequently proposed a three-phase strategy. In Phase I, over a period of four to six weeks, the United States would expand the armed reconnaissance effort over the North except for the sanctuary areas and again attack previously struck JCS-numbered targets in the northeast. Air units also would strike 11 more JCS-numbered bridges, and the Thai Nguyen railroad yards and shops; perform armed reconnaissance over Kep airfield; strike 30 more JCS-numbered targets, 14 headquarters/barracks, four ammunition and two supply depots, five POL storage areas, one airfield, two naval bases, and one radar site.

In Phase II, a period of somewhat less duration than Phase I, American aircraft would attack 12 military and war-supporting targets within the reduced sanctuary areas, consisting of two bridges, three POL storage areas, two railroad shops and yards, three supply and storage depots, one machine tool plant, and one airfield. During Phase III all remaining JCS-numbered targets (now totaling 43) would be attacked, including six bridges, seven ports and naval bases, six industrial plants, seven locks, 10 thermal/hydroelectric plants, the headquarters of the North Vietnamese ministries of national and air defense, and specified railroad, supply, radio, and transformer stations.

Concurrent with this program, the study group proposed three attack options that could be executed at any time: Option A, strike the Haiphong POL center; Option B, mine the channel approaches to Haiphong, Hon Gai, and Cam Pha; and Option C, strike four jet airfields -- at Phuc Yen, Hanoi, and Haiphong.

Finally, it proposed that Admiral Sharp should determine when to hit the targets in each of the three phases, the weight of the air attacks, and the tactics to be employed.[17]

General Wheeler, who was briefed on the report on 9 April, called it a "fine professional approach," a "good job," and endorsed it. The manner in which it should be sent to Secretary McNamara created difficulties, however. General McConnell suggested that the Joint Staff prepare "positive" recommendations for the implementation of the report's air program, stating that if this were not done, it would not receive the attention it deserved. But strong service support was lacking for that approach. An agreement eventually was reached to send the report to

Secretary McNamara with the Joint Chiefs "noting" it. They advised him it was fully responsive to his request, was in consonance with the JCS recommendations of 18 January 1966, and would be useful in considering future recommendations of the Rolling Thunder program.[18]

Air Operations in May: Beginning of "Gate Guard"

(U) The Rolling Thunder study had no immediate impact on air operations. In fact, Secretary Brown on 22 May publicly affirmed the administration's decision not to expand significantly attacks on new targets. He said such action would not cut off infiltration but would raise the danger of a wider war.*[19]

Thus the authorized level of 5,100 sorties for North Vietnam remained unchanged in May and only a few important attacks on fixed targets were approved. The principal operation was against seven targets within the Yen Bai logistic center which were struck by 70 USAF sorties. Monsoon weather again plagued the air campaign, causing the cancellation of 2,972 USAF-Navy sorties or about 32 percent of those scheduled. USAF sortie cancellations amounted to 40 percent.[20]

Heavier North Vietnamese infiltration toward the DMZ as indicated by more truck sightings led to a change in tactics. Beginning on 1 May, a special air effort called "Gate Guard" was initiated in the northern part of the Steel Tiger area in Laos and then shifted into route package I when the monsoons hit the Laotian region. Utilizing many of the "integrated interdiction" tactics developed in Laos earlier in the year, Gate Guard involved stepped-up air strikes on a series of routes or "belts"

---
* Not stated by Secretary Brown was the fact that civil disturbances in South Vietnam triggered by the dismissal of General Thi on 10 March still prompted the administration not to risk escalation of the war at this time. See p 18.

running east to west. Many special USAF aircraft were used: C-130 airborne command and control centers, C-130 flare aircraft, EB-66's for ECM, and RF-101's. Attack aircraft interdicted selected points in daytime and destroyed "fleeting targets" at night.[21]

During the month there were few MIG sightings and only one was destroyed. Heavy antiaircraft fire accounted for most of the 20 U.S. aircraft (13 USAF, six Navy, one Marine) that were downed. USAF losses included seven F-105's in the northeast. The enemy's ground fire, General McConnell informed a Senate subcommittee during the month, was "the only thing we are not able to cope with . . ." whereas the SA-2's -- which were deployed at about 103 sites -- had destroyed only five USAF and two Navy aircraft. The SA-2's were countered by decoys, jamming techniques, and evasive aircraft tactics.*[22]

During May the Air Staff began a study effort to establish requirements for a suitable, night, all-weather aircraft interdiction system using the latest munitions, sensors, and guidance equipment to provide an "aerial blockade" against infiltrating men and supplies. This followed an expression of frustration by high State Department and White House officials in late April about the inability of air power to halt these movements into the South. As part of this study, the Air Staff solicited the views of PACAF, SAC, and other commands, advising them of the need for a solution within existing bombing restraints. Recommendations to "strike the source" of Communist supplies, they were informed, were politically unacceptable and likely to remain so.[23]

---
* Air Force confidence in the value of anti-SA-2 operations was challenged in a Seventh Fleet study, dated 12 July 1966 and based on SA-2 USAF and Navy firing reports. It asserted that the value of ECM and other jamming techniques was uncertain as aircraft with deception devices normally sought to evade the missiles when fired upon. For General Harris' view, see pp 53-54.

In a joint reply on 24 May, the commanders-in-chief of PACAF and SAC, Generals Hunter Harris, Jr. and John D. Ryan, pointed to improved results from air operations in route package I and in parts of Laos. They said that interdiction could become even more effective by greater use of air-delivered mines (against ferries), "denial" munitions with delayed fuzes insuring "longevity" up to 30 days, around-the-clock air strikes on selected routes south of Vinh, special strikes against Mugia Pass, and improved air-ground activity in Laos. They also proposed the use of low-volatile chemical-biological agents to contaminate terrain and surface bursts of nuclear weapons. The latter would "dramatically" create "barriers" in areas difficult to by-pass. To implement these measures, General Harris again stressed the need for centralized control of air resources, asserting it should be a "high priority" Air Force objective. But most of these suggestions could not or would not be implemented in the immediate future.[24]

Highlights of June Operations

June witnessed another step-up in air activity over North Vietnam, the major highlight being USAF-Navy strikes, beginning 21 June, against previously exempt POL storage sites and culminating in major POL strikes in Hanoi and Haiphong on the 29th. (See details in Chapter III.)

Other targets continued to be hit, such as the Hanoi-Lao Cai and Hanoi-Dong Dang rail lines, but most USAF sorties concentrated on route package I targets which absorbed about 93 percent of the total flown in the North that month. These strikes reflected the importance General Westmoreland placed on curbing the flow of enemy troops and supplies toward and into the DMZ. Gate Guard targets were hit hard and, after the introduction of USAF MSQ-77 "Skyspot" radars for greater bombing accuracy,* the infiltration "gates" were "guarded" virtually around the clock. About 97 percent of the Navy effort was concentrated along the coast in route packages II, III, and IV. The VNAF flew 266 sorties in route package I, its highest total against the North in 12 months.[25]

The Gate Guard campaign seemed to confirm the value of night air attacks. By 7 July the nightime missions had achieved better results than those in daytime, 164 trucks being destroyed and 265 damaged compared with the daytime toll of 154 destroyed and 126 damaged.[26]

Despite these successes, Gate Guard operations faced certain handicaps. During daylight hours USAF 0-1 forward air control (FAC) aircraft -- used to support U.S. strikes -- were highly vulnerable to the heavy ground fire and, when forced to fly higher, became less effective. Also, interdiction points, often on flat terrain, were easy to repair or by-pass. And the North Vietnamese could store and service their trucks in numerous small villages, secure in the knowledge that U.S. aircraft would not attack civilian areas. Events finally overtook the Gate Guard effort. Continued infiltration through the DMZ prompted Headquarters MACV to develop a "Tally-Ho" air program -- a more ambitious effort to block, if possible, a large-scale invasion by North Vietnamese troops through the DMZ into South Vietnam's northernmost provinces.[27]

---

* The initial MSQ-77 radar was placed at Bien Hoa, South Vietnam on 1 April 1966, and the second one at Pleiku in May. With the installation of the third and fourth radars at Nakhon Phanom, Thailand and Dong Ha, South Vietnam on 3 and 12 June, respectively, the system could be used for air strikes in route package I. A fifth radar was placed at Dalat, South Vietnam on 26 September. The MSQ-77 was an MSQ-35 bomb-scoring radar converted into a bomb-directing radar with a range of 200 nautical miles.

III. THE POL STRIKES AND ROLLING THUNDER PROGRAM 51

As indicated, the highlight of the air war -- and of the Rolling Thunder program since its inception -- were the POL strikes in June 1966. General McConnell and the other service chiefs had long urged the destruction of North Vietnam's major POL sites but the administration did not seriously consider attacking them until March.

Background of the POL Air Strikes

Some months before, in December 1965, a CIA study had concluded that the destruction of the North's POL facilities would substantially increase Hanoi's logistic problems by requiring alternate import and distributing channels and the use of more rail cars, drums, and other storage items. CIA analysts recognized that the North Vietnamese probably anticipated such attacks and that the POL facilities near Haiphong, a major port city, politically were sensitive targets. Assessing the consequences of a POL air campaign, they further concluded it would (1) not change Hanoi's policy either toward negotiation or toward sharply entering the war; (2) probably result in more Soviet pressure on the regime to negotiate; (3) force Hanoi to ask for and receive more supply and transport aid from China and air defense aid from the Soviet Union; (4) aggravate Soviet-Chinese relations, and (5) cause further deterioration of U.S.-Soviet relations, especially if a Soviet ship were hit. Soviet counteraction was thought possible and might take the form of attacks on U.S. ferrett aircraft or interference with U.S. access to West Berlin. Chinese Communist intervention in the war, while possible, was considered unlikely.[1]

In March another CIA study predicted that the destruction of POL sites (and a cement plant in Haiphong) would severely strain the North's transportation system. It was one of the most influential documents to bear on the subject. On 23 March Secretary McNamara informed General Wheeler that a new Rolling Thunder program directed against POL storage and distribution targets might be favorably received. On 25 April, Deputy Secretary of Defense Cyrus R. Vance assured the JCS that its 1965 POL studies were now receiving full consideration. On 6 May, a White House aide, Walt W. Rostow, recalling the impact of oil strikes on Germany in World War II, suggested to the Secretaries of State and Defense that systematic and sustained bombing of POL targets might have more prompt and decisive results on Hanoi's transportation system than conventional intelligence indicated.* [2]

On 31 May -- although a final decision to hit the major facilities had not been made -- Admiral Sharp was authorized to attack certain POL-associated targets in the northeast along with five small route targets. On 6 June General Westmoreland advised CINCPAC that an improving political situation in South Vietnam (since civil disturbances began on 10 March) was causing Hanoi much disappointment and dismay. Noting this circumstance and the heavy toll inflicted by the air campaign over North Vietnam and Laos, he recommended that these psychological and military gains be "parlayed into dividends" by hitting the POL storage sites. To do so later, he warned, would be less effective because of dispersal work already under way. [3]

Support continued to build up. Admiral Sharp quickly endorsed General Westmoreland's views and, on 8 June, the U.S. Ambassador

---
* Mr. Rostow observed that in 1965 U.S. estimates showed that 60 percent of the North's POL was for military purposes and 40 percent for civilian needs. The current ratio was now placed at 80 and 20 percent, respectively.

to South Vietnam, Henry Cabot Lodge suggested that intensified bombing was the most effective way to get Hanoi to the negotiating table. General McConnell, who had long supported such action, told a Senate subcommittee that hitting POL targets would have a "substantial" effect on the amount of supplies the Communists could send to their forces in South Vietnam. An Air Staff intelligence report asserted that hitting the sites would have "a most profound" impact on Hanoi's infiltration activities and expressed confidence it could be done without causing severe civilian casualties.[4]

The Strikes of 29 June

The administration now moved toward its decision. In a preliminary action, the JCS on 16 June authorized Admiral Sharp to hit all of the POL dispersal sites listed in the current Rolling Thunder program except those within a 30-nautical-mile radius of Hanoi, a 10-nautical-mile radius of Haiphong, and 25 nautical miles from the Chinese border east of longitude 105° 20' E. and 30 nautical miles west of longitude 105° 20' E. On 21 June USAF jets struck gasoline and oil depot sites ranging from 28 to 40 miles from Hanoi. Several other sites, previously exempt from attack, were hit in ensuing days outside the Hanoi-Haiphong area.[5]

In addition, extraordinary steps were taken to prepare for the attacks on POL targets in the two main cities of North Vietnam. On 23 June, after Secretary McNamara and General Wheeler had informed President Johnson of their precautionary measures* to avoid attacks on civilian areas

---
* Nine "rules" were laid down: use of pilots most experienced with operations in the target areas, weather conditions permitting visual target identification, avoiding to the extent possible populated areas, minimum pilot distraction to improve delivery accuracy, use of munitions assuring highest precision consistent with mission objectives, attacks on air defenses only in sparsely populated areas, special security precautions concerning the proposed operations, and personnal attention by commanders to the operations.

and foreign merchant ships, the JCS authorized Admiral Sharp to strike early on the 24th seven POL storage facilities and a radar site at Kep, northeast of Hanoi. Although special security precautions surrounded the planning, the news media soon reported the essential details of the operation. This forced the administration to postpone it and deny any decision had been made.[6]

The strike was rescheduled and took place on 29 June. A USAF force of 24 F-105's, 8 F-105 "Iron Hand's", 4 EB-66's plus 24 F-4C's and 2 F-104's for MIG "cap" and escort hit a 32-tank farm about three-and-a-half miles from Hanoi. Approximately 95 percent of the target area, comprising about 20 percent of the North's oil storage facilities, was damaged or destroyed. Simultaneously, Navy A-4 and A-6 aircraft hit a large POL storage area two miles northwest of Haiphong. This facility, containing an estimated 40 percent of the North's fuel storage capacity and 95 percent of its unloading equipment, was about 80 percent destroyed. One USAF F-105 was lost to ground fire. Four MIG-17's challenged the raiders and one was probably shot down by an Iron Hand F-105. No SA-2 missiles were observed. Maj. Gen. Gilbert L. Myers, deputy commander of the Seventh Air Force termed the raids "the most significant, the most important strike of the war." Secretary McNamara subsequently called the USAF-Navy strike "a superb professional job," although he was highly incensed over the security leaks that preceded the attacks.[7]

(U) In a press conference the next day, the defense chief said the strikes were made "to counter a mounting reliance by North Vietnam on the use of trucks and powered junks to facilitate the infiltration of men and equipment from North Vietnam to South Vietnam." He explained that truck movements in the first five months of 1966 had doubled, and that daily supply tonnage and troop infiltration over the "Ho Chi Minh trail" were up 150 percent and 120 percent, respectively, over 1965. Further, the enemy had built new roads and its truck inventory by December 1966 was expected to be double that of January 1965. This would require a 50- to 70-percent increase in oil imports over 1965. The Secretary also justified the timing of the strikes, asserting that the "perishable" nature of POL targets made it more desirable to attack them now than earlier in the year.[8]

President Johnson said that the air strikes on military targets in North Vietnam "will continue to impose a growing burden and a high price on those who wage war against the freedom of others." He directed that in the forthcoming weeks first priority be given to "strangling" the remainder of Hanoi's POL system except for that portion in areas still exempt from air attack. He also wanted more bombing of the two main rail lines running between Hanoi and China.[9]

The Mid-1966 Assessment

Shortly after the 29 June POL strikes, another major conference took place in Honolulu to review the war and plan additional U.S. and allied air, ground, and naval deployments. A mid-year assessment of the war, contained in a letter from Admiral Sharp to the JCS and the Office of the Secretary of Defense (OSD), was expanded in briefings for Mr. McNamara in Honolulu on 8 July. The PACOM commander said that he considered the air program for North Vietnam still inadequate, observing that previous recommendations to hit major ports of entry, logistic targets leading from China, and certain POL sites (in addition to those struck on 29 June) had not been approved. He thought it impossible to prevent the enemy from moving supplies from North to South and thus to "isolate the battlefield"; rather, the "highest task" was route interdiction and striking new targets as they were uncovered. Recent intelligence showed that the air campaign was hurting Hanoi. Its repair and reconstruction force now totaled about 500,000 and the morale of the government and troops was declining. To raise the cost of infiltration, he proposed striking as soon as possible 33 important exempted targets and more of the enemy's supplies, road and rail repair centers, and military training areas.[10]

Admiral Sharp pointed to Hanoi's greater effort to hide and disperse its logistic supplies because of the air attacks. As a result there was greater U.S. effort in the first six months of the year to uncover more of the following types of targets:

	1 Jan 66	1 Jul 66	Total New Targets
Truck Parks	55	126	121
Military Storage Facilities	316	696	380
POL	38	180	142
Military Installations	680	939	259
Transshipment Points	7	65	65
Total	1,096	2,006	967

The table showed an increase of 90 percent in significant targets since 1 January 1966 with the major portion consisting of truck parks, military storage facilities, and transshipment points.

During the first half of the year, Admiral Sharp continued, Rolling Thunder strikes had destroyed or damaged 1,076 trucks, 900 pieces of rolling stock, and 3,304 watercraft. A total of 2,771 trucks were destroyed or damaged in Laos. Discussing the North's air defense system, he said that Hanoi's antiaircraft gun inventory had increased from about 859 in February 1965 (when the bombings began) to more than 4,200,[*] an average increase of about 205 guns per month. The North also possessed 20 to 25

---
[*] See pp16 and 63-65, and app 8.

active SA-2 battalions, good early warning, ground control interception equipment, and a respectable MIG force.[11]

In reply, Secretary McNamara reported that President Johnson had accorded first priority to "strangulation" of the North's POL system. Thus, it was essential to determine Hanoi's land and sea distribution system, categorize the targets, and then render them ineffective. The Secretary also pointed out the need for increased interdiction of railroad lines, particularly bridges in the northeast and northwest leading to China. Expressing concern over U.S. aircraft attrition, he said OSD was working with the services on ways to reduce it.[12]

The Beginning of Rolling Thunder Program 51

The strangulation campaign was incorporated into a new Rolling Thunder program -- number 51. It was authorized by the JCS on 6 July and went into effect on the 9th. Armed reconnaissance could now encompass all of North Vietnam except for the established sanctuary areas (i.e., a 30-nautical-mile radius of Hanoi, a 10-nautical-mile radius of Haiphong, and 25 to 30-nautical-mile buffer area adjacent to China). Admiral Sharp assigned PACAF specific responsibility for halting all rail traffic in the northeast and northwest sectors. In addition, the JCS on 9 July authorized an increase in attack sorties for North Vietnam and Laos from 8,100 to 10,100 per month.[13]

Because of the high priority assigned to the strangulation effort -- and in response also to Secretary McNamara's direction -- the Air Staff on 16 July established an Operation Combat Strangler task force headed by Maj. Gen. Woodrow P. Swancutt, Director of Operations, Headquarters USAF. Its immediate objective was to evaluate POL strangulation and LOC interdiction plans prepared by the Seventh Air Force and PACAF. Simultaneously, the Air Staff established an Operations Review Group within the Directorate of Operations under Col. LeRoy J. Manor, an enlarged and reorganized successor to the ad hoc study group formed on 26 March 1965.* It examined the effectiveness of combat and combat support operations in Southeast Asia as well as the activities of USAF worldwide operational forces.[14]

Under Rolling Thunder program 51, USAF aircraft intially concentrated on route packages I, V, and VIA and the Navy on the others. Then on 20 July, at the direction of General Westmoreland, the Air Force inaugurated a "Tally-Ho" air campaign in route package I in a renewed effort, somewhat similar to Gate Guard, to curb Communist infiltration into and through the DMZ. Also, on 6 August at General Westmoreland's request and by the decision of Admiral Sharp, the "Dixie Station" aircraft carrier used for air operations in South Vietnam was moved to "Yankee Station," thereby providing three rather than two carriers for the stepped up air activities against the North. Another important change was an agreement between the Seventh Air Force and Seventh Fleet commanders whereby the former would provide about 1,500 sorties per month in the normally Navy-dominated route packages II, III, and IV. The Air Staff and General Harris considered the arrangement better than the relatively rigid delineation of service air responsibility for the North that had existed previously. Although the agreement took effect on 4 September+, restrictions on air operations east of "route 15" prevented its full realization.++ [15]

---

* See p 16.

+ By September USAF aircraft generally were covering 46,265 square miles or 77 percent of the land area of North Vietnam. The Navy, by comparison, was covering 13,891 square miles or about 23 percent of the land area.

++ The restrictions were eased in December 1966.

The immediate priority, of course, was given to POL sites. The campaign increased in momentum until the week of 13-19 August when 140 attack sorties were flown against POL targets. Thereafter the sortie rate dropped. By the end of August an estimated 68 percent of known POL storage capacity in route packages I, V, and VI had been destroyed. On 19 September the remaining POL capacity in the North was placed at about 69,650 metric tons, of which 18,526 metric tons were not yet authorized for destruction.[16]

By the end of September it was apparent that the POL strikes were becoming less productive. There had been no let-up in Soviet deliveries of POL supplies and the North Vietnamese continued their dispersal efforts. Supported by Combat Strangler analyses, PACAF considered the benefits derived from attacking the scattered sites no longer worth the cost in aircraft lost. In a report to Secretary Brown on 14 October, PACAF stated that the POL campaign had reached the point of diminishing returns and that the Soviet Union and China could adequately supply the North with POL products. Also, U.S. air power could best force changes in POL handling and distribution by striking targets listed in Rolling Thunder program 52 proposed by the JCS on 22 August.* This would constitute, PACAF felt, the best kind of "strategic persuasion" before Hanoi could devise countermeasures.[17]

The railroad strangulation effort, particularly against the Hanoi-Lao Cai and the Hanoi-Dong Dang lines running to China and located in route packages V and VI A, was not especially productive because of bad weather and the ability of the North Vietnamese to repair the lines quickly. In fact,

---

* This program called for 872 sorties over 19 new targets.

PACAF believed it was virtually impossible to maintain an effective air program against them. Weather problems in the two route packages forced the cancellation or diversion of about 70 and 81 percent of the attack sorties scheduled for July and August, respectively. The weather improved in September but turned poor again in October.[18]

Enemy antiaircraft defense, including additional SA-2's also added to the difficulty in interdicting the two main rail lines. As American aircraft losses rose, Admiral Sharp on 20 September ordered a reduction of about one-third of the air strikes in route package VIA until measures could be devised to reduce the toll. For example, on 7 August antiaircraft guns knocked down seven U.S. aircraft (six USAF, one Navy), the highest one-day total since 13 August 1965 when six were shot down. American combat losses in the North during the third quarter of the year were: 41 in July, 37 in August, and 26 in September. Eighty of these were USAF aircraft. In October combat losses declined to 23, only nine of them USAF.[19]

MIG pilots also became increasingly aggressive. Fifteen "incidents" in July resulted in two MIG-21's and one MIG-17 being shot down against the loss of one USAF F-105 and one Navy F-8. During an engagement on 7 July, two MIG-21's for the first time in the war fired air-to-air missiles against two F-105's but failed to score. Another milestone in the air war occurred on 21 September when the biggest air-to-air battle to date was fought over the North. In seven separate encounters USAF pilots downed two MIG-17's, probably a third, and damaged a MIG-21 without suffering any losses.[20]

The Tally-Ho Campaign

In terms of total sorties flown, the largest portion of the USAF effort, as in previous months, was concentrated in route package I which included the DMZ, the area of the greatest enemy threat. Intelligence believed that about 5,000 North Vietnamese had infiltrated through the zone in June. PACAF speculated that these enemy movements may have been due to the recent success of Tiger Hound air operations in Laos which, together with monsoon weather, had virtually blocked certain logistic routes in that country.[21]

As more enemy troops pressed toward the DMZ and intelligence reported that the North's 324 "B" Division of 8,000 to 10,000 men, had crossed over into the I Corps area of South Vietnam, General Westmoreland asked Lt. Gen. William W. Momyer, who succeeded General Moore as Seventh Air Force commander on 1 July, to prepare an air program similar to Tiger Hound in Laos for the most southern part of route package I including the zone. Already under way just south of the DMZ was a combined U.S. Marine and South Vietnamese Army and Marine air and ground effort called Operation Hastings. General Momyer quickly outlined a "Tally-Ho" air campaign against enemy targets in an area about 30 miles inside North Vietnam from the Dai Giang river below Dong Hoi through the DMZ to its southern border. The first Tally-Ho air strike was made on 20 July by USAF and Marine aircraft, the latter beginning regular operations in the North for the first time.* Like Gate Guard, C-130 airborne control was employed and, for the first time, USAF O-1 FAC's flew into North Vietnam to help find targets. To sustain Tally-Ho, Tiger Hound activity in Laos was scaled down.[22]

Although Tally-Ho included the DMZ, military operations

---
* Previously Marine Corps activities in the North consisted of eight sorties in April and two sorties in June.

within the zone were not conducted immediately. The political problems associated with such action had been under study for some time. On 20 July, the day Tally-Ho began, the JCS finally authorized Admiral Sharp to launch air or artillery strikes in the southern half of the zone. This followed protracted State and Defense Department negotiations which resulted in State's approval if the allies had concrete evidence that the North was using the zone for infiltrating men and materiel, if there existed an adequate record of the Saigon government's protest to the International Control Commission (ICC)* concerning Hanoi's violation of the zone, and if an appropriate public affairs program was begun prior to military action in the zone.[23]

After these conditions were fulfilled, the JCS on 28 July specifically authorized B-52 strikes in the southern portion of the DMZ in support of U.S.-South Vietnamese "self-defense" operations. In their first attack there, on 30 July, 15 B-52's dropped bombs on ammunition dumps, gun positions, and weapon staging targets. In August B-52's returned there several times.[24]

On 22 August General McConnell informed Secretaries Vance and McNamara of a rising trend in USAF out-of-country night operations, especially in North Vietnam, and of his expectation that the trend would continue in the Tally-Ho campaign. But shortly thereafter the hazards of antiaircraft fire and inadequate aircraft control forced a reduction in the use of USAF 0-1 FAC's and, consequently, of other combat aircraft. In fact, the night attack effort, despite General McConnell's hopes, did not show a significant rise again until December.[25]

---

* The ICC, composed of representatives from India, Canada, and Poland, was established in July 1954 as a result of the Geneva conference that ended the French-Indochina war. Its primary function was to supervise the 1954 Geneva agreements.

In September the advent of better weather and better results with the use of MSQ-77 radar permitted intensification of the Tally-Ho operations. Many secondary explosions often followed USAF-Marine Corps air strikes. The first B-52 strike in the northern portion of the DMZ was made on 16 September and others soon followed until 26 September when they were halted in the zone east of route package I to permit ICC inspection of North Vietnamese troop infiltration. As the Communists continued to use this area, administration authorities on 13 October rescinded the prohibition against air and artillery strikes. On the 14th B-52 strikes were stopped in the zone, this time because of the danger from suspected SA-2 sites.[26]

Tally-Ho continued through October and into November. As in the Gate Guard operations, Tally-Ho FAC pilots often were forced up to 1,500 feet by ground fire, thus reducing the value of visual reconnaissance. They also experienced severe turbulence over mountainous terrain and poor weather added to their difficulties.[27]

The Tally-Ho program remained under constant review. Initial evidence appeared to show that its operations destroyed many enemy structures, supplies, antiaircraft positions, and vehicles, and that it hampered but did not stop infiltration on foot through the DMZ. On 10 October, during a briefing for Secretary McNamara and other top officials who were visiting Saigon, Brig. Gen. Carlos M. Talbott of the Seventh Air Force indicated that Tally-Ho and other air activities possibly had caused the enemy to reach the limit of his supply capability. PACAF officials thought that Tally-Ho and U.S.-South Vietnamese "spoiling" attacks in and below the DMZ had thwarted a major offensive planned by the North Vietnamese into the I Corps. On the 13th, the JCS, in answer to a White House request for an assessment of the enemy threat in the zone, likewise reported that spoiling attacks and tactical and

B-52 air strikes in and near the demilitarized area had defeated the North Vietnamese and prevented them from seizing the initiative. But the service chiefs warned that the enemy still retained considerable offensive capability and that U.S. reinforcements should be sent to that region.[28]

However, these were general observations. The USAF Vice Chief of Staff, Gen. Bruce K. Holloway, when pressed by Secretary Brown on the effect of the air effort on North Vietnamese movement through the DMZ, was less certain about the results of Tally-Ho operations. He replied: "I do not know what the effect is and nobody else seems to know," adding that there was much "speculation and excuses why it's hard to determine." He said that there were several actions under way to improve data-gathering in the DMZ area. These included establishing a tactical air support analysis team (TASAT) composed of 20 Air Force and Army personnel to insure systematic data-reporting, forming a similar USAF-Army team to assess B-52 strikes, inviting the Army and Navy to join the Air Force Combat Strangler task force in assessing the results of the air campaign, and organizing an air weapon survey board.[29]

The need for more reliable information on Tally-Ho activities near the DMZ was also reflected in the observation of a USAF intelligence officer in South Vietnam who was associated with the air campaign. "We don't know how effective we were," he commented, "for we don't know what we stopped or the amount of flow." He thought the program could be made more productive by defoliating the terrain and by improving intelligence, targeting, and communication procedures. Subsequently, a list of targets believed to have been damaged or destroyed by the Tally-Ho program was compiled.*[30]

---

* See p 62.

IV. ANALYSES OF THE AIR CAMPAIGN

The beginning of Rolling Thunder program 51 also witnessed the start of a greater Air Staff effort to analyze the effectiveness of USAF operations in Southeast Asia, particularly in North Vietnam. With the assignment of more personnel in July to the Operations Review Group under Colonel Manor and Operation Combat Strangler under General Swancutt, the Air Force improved its ability to collect and evaluate operational data and to respond to requests from higher authorities for information on different aspects of the air war.

Operational Studies

One of the early important products of the Swancutt task force was its analysis of the Seventh Air Force POL and LOC air campaign against North Vietnam. Completed on 30 August, it pointed to the inflexibility of air operations in the North. This situation was attributed to seven main factors: air restrictions that reduced aircraft maneuver, the prohibition against striking certain target areas, the "route package" system that divided into relatively independent regions the USAF and Navy target areas of responsibility, a targeting system that had the effect of concentrating air power and thus "telegraphing" U.S. intentions to the enemy, bad weather and anti-aircraft defenses that left little choice in tactics, the existence of few profitable targets, and fragmented command and control of air activities.

Based upon its analysis, the task force recommended two primary changes: a broadened target base to allow an increase in the tempo of air operations and a single centralized command and control system for air. It also began assembling a complete statistical record of aircraft losses, ordnance expended, results of air strikes, and tactics employed (because of the inordinately high aircraft losses in route packages V and VIA), and analyzing Seventh Air Force and PACAF plans weekly. The group also proposed that the Air Force seek permission for its aircraft to hit targets in the Navy-dominated route packages II, III, and IV when weather forced diversionary strikes, and it recommended more night air operations. Agreements subsequently were reached to allow USAF units to make diversionary air strikes in the Navy areas, the new policy becoming effective on 4 September.[1]

Also in August the Air Staff examined the value of air attacks on North Vietnamese watercraft. This was in response to a query from Secretary Brown who observed that Admiral Sharp, in his briefing of 8 July in Honolulu, had indicated that 2,358 watercraft had been attacked by air to that time.[2] General Holloway advised on 22 August that in Admiral Sharp's view, air strikes on largely coastal watercraft through mid-1966 had not always been worth the effort, although they did have a harassing effect on the North Vietnamese. Since July, because of the stepped up air operations on land transportation routes, a larger volume of barge traffic had appeared on inland waterways. In the Thanh Hoa and Vinh areas, watercraft construction was exceeding civilian needs. Some watercraft carried POL drums, tanks, and ammunition, and there were more attempts to camouflage them. Thus, said General Holloway, Admiral Sharp now believed that they were worthwhile air targets.[3]

On 13 September, again at the request of Secretary Brown, the Air Staff undertook a detailed study of the types of target systems in North Vietnam. The approach included an examination of the cost and the length of time needed to destroy a part or all of each target, and the effect its loss would have on Hanoi's ability to continue hostilities. The primary target systems being studied were electric power, maritime ports, airfields, navigation locks and dams, industrial facilities, command and control sites, extractive industries, military installations, and LOC's. The project had not been completed by the end of the year.[4]

The Effectiveness of Air Power

The Air Staff also assembled data to reply to numerous questions raised by Secretary McNamara on the effectiveness of air power. On 2 September, during a meeting with Air Force, Navy, and other officials, the defense chief asked the Air Force to examine the combat use of F-4C and F-105 aircraft. He wished to determine whether F-4C's should fly most of the sorties against North Vietnam, especially against "fleeting" night targets, and whether F-105's should be employed in South rather than North Vietnam. He also asked for a comparative study of the performance of propeller and jet aircraft in night operations over route packages I and II. From the Navy, Secretary McNamara wanted recommendations on how to increase the number of night sorties over North Vietnam.[5]

On the basis of data collected by the Air Staff, Secretary Brown advised the defense chief on 28 September that while the F-4C and F-105 aircraft were both suited for daytime attack missions, the F-4C was more effective at night, principally because it carried two pilots. This permitted better target-finding, better radar-controlled formations (by the rear pilot), and more protection for pilots against "spatial disorientation/vertigo." Although a switch in the use of the F-105 from North to South Vietnam would reduce its losses, other reasons militated against such a change. It would affect the logistical base of the two aircraft, probably not reduce aircraft attrition in route package areas V and VI (where enemy defenses were heaviest), and create an aircrew replacement problem. He supported the assigned missions of the two aircraft and the practice of "attriting" the F-105's first in order to conserve the F-4C's.

Secretary Brown reported that comparisons between propeller and jet aircraft in night operations were inconclusive because of vast differences in their use. In North Vietnam the Air Force used its A-1's in less defended areas while the Navy did not employ its A-1's until an area was first tested by A-4's. In Laos Air Force A-1 losses were higher because of lower attack speed or more ordnance-delaying passes against targets.[6]

The study requested by Secretary McNamara on stepping up night operations over North Vietnam was submitted by Navy Secretary Paul M. Nitze. He said more night sorties would cause a drop of about 15 percent in Navy attack efforts, reduce effectiveness by about 50 percent compared with daytime strikes, result in more civilian casualties, and double operational aircraft losses -- although combat losses would remain about the same. In view of these findings, and because he believed it was necessary to maintain pressure on the North "around the clock," Secretary Nitze recommended no change in the current "mix" of day and night sorties.[7]

Secretary McNamara also expressed dissatisfaction with the level of air analysis performed by the services, pointing to the differences between the estimates made in several studies on the effects that the POL strikes would have on North Vietnamese infiltration and those that actually occurred. He asked the Navy Secretary especially to review past CIA, DIA, and other reports on this matter as well as analyze the general subject of aircraft losses. He enjoined the Air Force to make more "sophisticated" analyses of the conflict, asserting that this was one of the "most important" things that it could do.[8]

On 3 November Secretary Nitze sent Mr. McNamara an initial report on the Navy's most recent air studies. The findings -- and admissions -- were unusual. He said the report showed that (1) there was insufficient intelligence data to produce a viable assessment of past or projected air campaigns; (2) North Vietnam's logistic requirements for forces in the South, compared with its capabilities, were small, thus permitting Hanoi to adjust the level of conflict to its available supplies; and (3) North Vietnam's estimated economic loss of $125 million versus $350 million of Soviet and Chinese aid taken alone, was a "poor trade-off" when compared with the cost of achieving the end product. The first two factors, the Navy Secretary observed, emphasized the magnitude of the task of disrupting North Vietnamese infiltration.

Admittedly, he continued, air attacks had produced some results such as requiring North Vietnam to provide for an air defense system and to maintain a 300,000-man road and bridge repair force that reduced resources available for infiltration into South Vietnam. And prisoner of war and defector reports testified to some success of the air and ground campaign in the South. Nevertheless, because of the inadequacy of available data, analysts were unable to develop a logical case for or against the current air campaign at either a higher or lower level. "This is not a criticism of the analytical effort," said Mr. Nitze, "rather, it is a reflection of the degree to which decisions in this area must be dependent on judgments in the absence of hard intelligence."

The Nitze report included a review of studies -- including the March 1966 CIA study which preceded and led to the U.S. decision to attack North Vietnam's POL system. The overall purpose of the air strikes had been to strain Hanoi's transportation system. Interviews with CIA analysts disclosed that many of their assumptions were based on certain estimates of the logistic capacity of the Hanoi-Dong Dang rail line, the amount of seaborne imports, the impact of hitting a cement plant in Haiphong, and other data. In retrospect, other factors also bore -- or could bear -- on the effectiveness of air operations against the enemy's logistic capability and resources, such as the existence of a road system parallel to the Hanoi-Dong Dang rail line, the construction by the Chinese of a new internal transport link to Lao Cai, the transport capacity of the Red River from Lao Cai to Hanoi, and the capability of the North Vietnamese to continue, although less efficiently, to produce cement in small, dispersed furnaces if the plant in Haiphong were destroyed.* There were indications that the analysts' use of 1965 average import statistics to project future North Vietnamese requirements resulted in an overstatement of Hanoi's needs. These -- and other examples -- showed the inadequacy of the information base for evaluating the effectiveness of air strike programs planned for North Vietnam.

To obtain better analyses for predicting the results of air strikes, the Nitze report indicated that the Chief of Naval Operations was establishing a special branch in the Navy's System Analysis Division to perform this vital task.[9]

---

* As the Haiphong plant was the only such facility in the North, the Air Staff seriously questioned the ability of the North Vietnamese to produce cement if it was destroyed.

Secretary Brown, in a reply to Mr. McNamara on 10 November, summarized current efforts to improve USAF analysis of the effectiveness of air interdiction. He cited the establishment in July of the Operation Combat Strangler task force and expansion of its functions to include development of a computer model to simulate air campaigns against North Vietnamese targets. The Air Force also was analyzing daily the air operations over North Vietnam, reviewing and evaluating major target systems including the anticipated effect of air attacks on the North's economy and on infiltration into the South, and studying the length of time required to destroy a given percentage of target systems and the cost of striking them in terms of sorties, munitions, and aircraft. This effort had been assigned top priority and the necessary resources. In addition to briefing the Air Staff, the task force made the various analyses available to the Joint Staff and OSD and posted pertinent data in a special situation room.

The Secretary of the Air Force also advised that the USAF study of major target systems in North Vietnam was 50 percent complete and would be finished early in 1967, after which a second analysis would "interface" all target systems to determine the cumulative effect of the destruction of several complimentary target systems. In addition, a special analysis of night operations was under way.[10]

Studies on Aircraft Attrition

Another problem area that received increased attention after mid-1966 was aircraft attrition. Following a USAF briefing on this subject on 6 June, Secretary McNamara asked the Air Force for a detailed analysis of losses.[11]

On 19 July Secretary Brown submitted coordinated USAF-Navy reply. Over North Vietnam, he said, the majority of aircraft losses (74 percent) were due to automatic weapon and light antiaircraft guns and most aircraft (77.1 percent) were hit below 4,000 feet. The losses were distributed fairly evenly over the route packages, with no meaningful differences in the loss rates by routes. He said an apparent USAF aircraft loss rate amounting to "three times" that of the Navy's was due principally to the lack of a clear definition of strike sorties, the limitations of the joint reporting system, and frequent diversion of sorties. Overall Air Force and Navy aircraft losses were quite similar, amounting to 3.96 and 4.32 aircraft per 1,000 sorties, respectively. He reported there was no data on the frequency of aircraft exposure to antiaircraft weapons at different altitudes, the proportion of losses sustained on each segment of an attack area, and the extent of increasing aircraft exposure to ground fire induced by avoiding SA-2 missiles.

An analysis of operational data for the period 1 October 1965 through 31 May 1966 by cause of loss, including "take-off" for combat missions, the Air Force Secretary continued, showed that by far most of the operational losses were due to aircraft system failures. The ratio of system failures to total operational losses in this period were by service: Air Force, 23 of 44; Navy, 10 of 29; and Marine Corps, three of nine. Of the 36 system failures, 22 involved aircraft engines, five were due to flight control problems, and the remainder were random system failures which occurred only once or twice. In addition, the Navy lost nine aircraft in carrier landings.

Compared with normal peacetime attrition, Secretary Brown added, actual operational losses in Southeast Asia for fiscal year 1966 were below predicted figures for USAF F-100's, F-104's, F-4C's and F-5's. Only F-105 losses were higher than expected and several efforts were under way, including a study by the Air Force Systems Command, to modify the aircraft in order to reduce combat losses. In addition to air crews, hydraulic-pneumatic systems (such as fuel and flight control) and aircraft engines were most vulnerable to enemy fire.[12]

At the request of Deputy Secretary Vance, the Air Force also made a special study of aircraft losses during night missions over North Vietnam and Laos. Reports submitted by Secretary Brown and General McConnell on 24 and 25 August showed that for the period 1 January - 31 July 1966, the aircraft loss rate per 1,000 sorties for night armed reconnaissance sorties averaged 0.84 compared to 4.27 for day armed reconnaissance. Night sorties were considerably less hazardous, primarily because North Vietnam's air defense weapons were largely optically directed.[13]

Aircraft losses remained of particular concern to the Air Staff since they threatened the Air Force's planned buildup to 86 tactical fighter squadrons by June 1968. On 29 August General Holloway, the Vice Chief of Staff, sent a report to General Wheeler on the effect of the losses on the Air Force's capabilities. It showed that at current aircraft loss rates the Air Force would be short five tactical fighter squadrons at the mid-point of fiscal year 1968 and three squadrons short at the end of the fiscal year. The approved squadron goal might not be reached until after the third quarter of fiscal year 1969. The report also indicated that an OSD-prepared aircraft "attrition model" needed adjustment to reflect more clearly sorties programmed for North Vietnam. It was on the basis of this model that OSD on 19 November 1965 had approved additional production of 141 F-4's to offset attrition. General Holloway said that the Air Staff would continue its analysis of this problem.[14]

(U) Aircraft attrition was, of course, being followed closely by administration officials and congressional critics. In recognition of the problem

Secretary McNamara on 22 September announced plans to procure in fiscal year 1968, 280 additional largely combat-type aircraft costing $700 million. Although the largest number were earmarked for the Navy, the Air Force would receive a substantial portion of the total.[15]

The Hise Report

Meanwhile, on 26 September, a Joint Staff study group completed a more detailed examination of aircraft attrition. Its findings were contained in the "Hise Report", named after the group's director, Marine Col. Henry W. Hise, whom General Wheeler had designated on 28 July to perform this task.*

The Hise group studied all factors affecting aircraft losses using data from joint operational reports, the DIA, and interviews with Air Force, Navy, and Marine commanders and airmen at Headquarters PACOM and in Southeast Asia. It covered all aircraft losses, whatever the cause, from January 1962 through August 1966. Totalling 814, the aircraft were lost in the following areas: North Vietnam, 363; Laos, 74; and South Vietnam, 377. The report analyzed the main factors affecting aircraft losses: time, enemy defenses, tactics, targeting, weather, sortie requirements, ordnance, aircrews, and stereotyped air operations.

The report's major conclusion was that North Vietnam had been given an opportunity to build up a formidable air defense system and noted, in support, General Momyer's recent observation: "In the past three months the enemy has moved to a new plateau of /air defense/ capability. He now has a fully integrated air defense system controlled from a central

---
* Some of the ground work of the Hise Report had been done by a study group headed by USAF Brig Gen. R.G. Owen at the request of General Wheeler on 25 April. The Hise study group consisted of four representatives -- one from each of the services, including USAF Col. C.L. Daniel -- and one representative from the DIA.

point in Hanoi." Both the antiaircraft guns and SA-2 missiles, according to the Hise Report, had had a "crippling effect" on air operations. The vast majority of aircraft losses were attributed to ground fire, with 85 percent of all "hits" being scored when the aircraft were below 4,500 feet. If Hanoi were permitted to continue its buildup of air defense weapons, the United States eventually would face a choice of supporting an adequate air campaign to destroy them, accepting high aircraft losses, or terminating air operations over the North.

The report also pointed to a number of other problems. It said that between 1 July and 15 September 1966 USAF's 354th TFS had experienced an inordinately high aircraft loss rate. Additionally, some pilots in the theater were overworked, several squadrons had fewer than authorized pilots, F-105 pilots had "low survivability" in route packages V and VIA, stereotyped operations contributed to air losses, and a larger stock of ordnance was needed to provide for a more intense antiflak program.[16]

General Harris on 20 October forwarded the PACAF-Seventh Air Force assessment of the Hise Report to General McConnell. He generally agreed with the report's conclusions about the buildup of the North's antiaircraft defenses and the need to broaden the target base. But he thought the report added little to a fundamental discussion of aircraft losses since it cited largely a number of well known facts. General Harris modified or took exception to a number of points raised. Concerning the effect of SA-2 missile (which forced pilots down to within range of antiaircraft guns), he said that Air Force "Wild Weasel" and "Iron Hand" forces* equipped with electronic

---

* Wild Weasel aircraft, largely F-100F's and F-105F's, were specially equipped for anti-SA-2 operations. Iron Hand was the operational code name for attacks on SA-2 sites.

countermeasures (ECM) equipment were mitigating the effect of the SA-2's on tactics*, although a major development effort was still needed in this area. In bad weather it was the lack of an all-weather bombing system that limited operations rather than SA-2's. The Soviet-made missiles merely complicated bombings, making it difficult for aircraft to fly higher lest they become vulnerable to a missile hit.[17]

With respect to high losses incurred by the 354th TFS, General Harris attributed this primarily to aggressive leadership, accidents, and misfortunes in only one squadron -- something that often happened in peace as well as in war without identifiable causes. Nor did he consider overwork or fatigue of pilots a factor in aircraft losses. F-105 pilots at Takhli and Korat Air Bases in Thailand, for example, in July flew an average of 56.7 and 43.9 hours respectively. In August they flew 48.2 and 36.5 hours respectively. Although aircraft often flew twice in one day, pilots seldom did except during "peak loads" and this was an infrequent requirement.

General Harris also took issue with a statistical interpretation showing that F-105 pilots flying 100 missions over route packages V and VIA would suffer excessive losses. Although the figures (based on July and August data) were approximately correct, they represented the greatest attrition rate in a period of maximum losses in the highest risk area in Southeast Asia. Seventh Air Force records showed that only 25 percent of pilot missions were in high risk areas. Thus, in a 100-mission tour, an F-105 pilot would not lose his aircraft over enemy or friendly territory as often as alleged. He further observed that the F-4C loss rate was about one-fourth that of the F-105 rate. He conceded that some squadrons at Takhli and

---

* For General McConnell's and the Seventh Fleet's view of the effectiveness of anti-SA-2 operations. See p 26.

Korat Air Bases had been below authorized pilot strength during the June-September period.

The PACAF commander also agreed that, to some extent, there was a tendency to use standard or "stereotyped" tactics because of the need for efficient air scheduling and to meet JCS objectives. But it was North Vietnam's effective early warning and ground control interception system rather than stereotyped tactics that aided the enemy and provided him with nearly total information on U.S. air operations. The advantages of existing air scheduling, he thought, far exceeded the disadvantages.[18]

The Air Staff and General McConnell considered the data in the Hise Report as accurate and generally accepted the findings. On 10 October the JCS informed Secretary McNamara that, to the extent possible, Admiral Sharp and the services had taken several steps to ameliorate the aircraft loss rate. But certain other measures would require administration approval, particularly increased production of specific types of munitions for more effective suppression of enemy air defenses. There included 2.75 rockets with M-151 heads, Shrikes, CBU-24's, and 2,000- and 3,000-pound bombs. The Joint Chiefs reaffirmed their recommendation of 22 August that Rolling Thunder program 52 be adopted to broaden the target base over North Vietnam and make possible increased destruction of enemy air defense sites.[19]

The Hise Report findings prompted Dr. Brown and Deputy Secretary of Defense Vance to seek clarification of certain aspects of aircraft attrition. Detailed replies subsequently were incorporated into a JCS paper in which the service chiefs also cited two major policy handicaps of the air war that contributed to aircraft losses. These were the administration's restrictive targeting policies and its observance of the sanctuary areas around

Hanoi, Haiphong, and in the buffer zone adjacent to China. They endorsed the Hise Report finding that North Vietnam's air defense system eventually could make air attacks unprofitable and reaffirmed the need for more ECM equipment and suitable ordnance. They disagreed with the report's belief that pilot fatigue contributed to losses, but conceded some pilots had been overworked because occasionally there were insufficient numbers of them. They pointed to Admiral Sharp's recent directive (of 2 October) stating that sorties allocated for North Vietnam and Laos were not mandatory figures to be achieved but were issued to indicate the weight of air effort that should go into certain areas. Air units were not to be pressed beyond a reasonable point.[20]

McNamara's Proposal to Reduce Aircraft Attrition

Meanwhile, based on a study by his Southeast Asia Program Division of 1965 aircraft loss rates, Secretary McNamara on 17 September sent the JCS a plan to reduce aircraft losses, particularly the Navy's. It took into consideration the Air Force's force structure which the division believed could absorb aircraft losses more easily. To reduce Navy losses, the Defense Secretary suggested shifting about 1,000 carrier sorties per month from North Vietnam and Laos to South Vietnam with the Air Force increasing its sortie activities in those two countries. He thought this might reduce Navy losses by about 59 aircraft during the next nine months. In absolute numbers, USAF losses had been less and Navy losses more than planned, in part because some "higher loss" targets initially planned for the Air Force had been assigned to the Navy. Loss rates varied widely by target. Overall, Mr. McNamara saw no significant difference in the air performance of the two services, asserting that "I think they're both doing a magnificent job and I see no difference as measured by loss rates in their effectiveness in combat."[21]

Generals McConnell and Harris strongly opposed any change in sortie assignments. So did the JCS which on 6 October replied by noting that differences between projected and actual aircraft losses in December 1965 had stemmed primarily from the high level of air effort in route packages V and VIA and the significant increase in enemy air defenses. The Joint Chiefs also observed that OSD had underestimated both total combat sorties to be flown over North Vietnam and Navy's noncombat aircraft losses. A shift in sorties to reduce losses would pose considerable operational difficulties for the Air Force by requiring more flying time and air refueling missions in order to reach the northernmost targets. The Navy too would have to make important operational adjustments.[22]

Affirming that every effort was being made to reduce aircraft and aircrew losses, the JCS again recommended Rolling Thunder program 52 as the best solution. It also noted that, under current projections, even with the recently announced (22 September) procurement increase,* new production would not equal aircraft losses.[23]

In view of this reply, Secretary McNamara abandoned plans to switch Air Force and Navy operational areas.

---

* See p 52.

V. THE AIR WAR AT YEAR'S END

While the Air Force concentrated on Tally-Ho strikes, the administration in late 1966 took another look at JCS proposals to increase the air pressure on North Vietnam. During a conference in October in Honolulu to review additional U.S. force deployments, Admiral Sharp proposed a revised strike program averaging 11,100 sorties per month against the North for 18 months beginning in January 1967. On 4 November the JCS endorsed both the deployment and sortie proposals and again advocated mining the sea approaches to North Vietnam's principal ports, as well as several other actions.[1]

On 8 November General Wheeler urged Secretary McNamara to approve the Rolling Thunder program 52 sent to him initially on 22 August. Except for some fixed targets, the program would prohibit armed reconnaissance within a 10-nautical-mile radius of Hanoi and Phuc Yen airfield and the Haiphong sanctuary would be limited to a radius of four nautical miles. The JCS chairman singled out a number of other major targets remaining in the North, commenting briefly on each. He proposed striking three SA-2 supply sites, observing that since 1 July 1965 at least 949 SA-2's had been launched against U.S. aircraft, destroying 32. He suggested attacks on certain POL storage facilities, estimating that 24,800 metric tons remained of an initial 132,000 metric tons of fixed POL storage capacity. Dispersed sites, he said, held about 42,500 metric tons. Other targets on his list included the Thai Nguyen steel plant, the Haiphong cement plant, two Haiphong power plants, four waterway locks (related to water transportation), and the port areas of Cam Pha and Haiphong.[2]

On 10 November Secretary Brown informed Secretary McNamara that he endorsed the proposed Rolling Thunder 52 program. It would include 472 strike sorties against selective targets (canal water locks, POL storage areas, manufacturing and electric power plants, and SA-2 support facilities) in route package areas V, VIA, and VIB. On the basis of 1 April - 30 September 1966 attrition rates, there would be a loss of eight aircraft. He thought the air strikes would reduce and discourage shipping operations, reduce POL storage, increase replenishment, repair, and construction problems, and make more difficult the resupply of Communist forces in the South.[3]

Approval of Rolling Thunder Program 52

The administration on 12 November approved a modified Rolling Thunder program 52. It contained 13 previously unauthorized JCS targets: a bridge, a railroad yard, a cement plant and two power plants in Haiphong, two POL facilities, two SA-2 supply sites, and selected elements of the Thai Nguyen steel plant. Ten vehicle depots also were earmarked for attack. To assure success of the overall program, the JCS raised the authorized attack sortie level to 13,200 per month for November. In separate but related planning action, Secretary McNamara limited the JCS-recommended air and ground deployment program through June 1968 on the grounds that an excessively large buildup could jeopardize some recently achieved economic stability in South Vietnam.[4]

Despite the new attack sortie authorization, the northeast monsoons restricted program "52" operations for the remainder of 1966. Actual sorties flown in November totaled 7,252 (3,681 USAF) and in December, 6,732 (USAF 4,129). These figures compared with the year's high of 12,154

U.S. attack sorties flown against the North in September. A sudden administration decision in November to defer striking six of the approved JCS targets also affected the sortie rate.[5]

Among the authorized targets were the Hai Gai POL storage site, hit on 22 November by USAF F-4C's, and the Dap Cai railroad bridge, a holdover from program "51". Navy aircraft struck the Haiphong SA-2 supply complex and the Cam Thon POL storage area. On 2 December USAF aircraft hit the Hoa Gai site for a second time while Navy aircraft conducted a first strike against the Van Vien vehicle depot. The latter was subsequently hit six times through 14 December. USAF aircraft also hit Yen Vien railroad year for the first time twice on 4 December and conducted restrikes on 13 and 14 December. Both the vehicle depot and the railroad yard were heavily damaged.[6]

The Furor Over Air Strikes "On Hanoi"

The USAF and Navy strikes of 13 and 14 December against the Van Vien vehicle depot and the Yen Vien railroad yard had international repercussions. The depot was about five nautical miles south of Hanoi and the yard, a major junction of three rail lines with two of them connecting with China, about six nautical miles northeast of Hanoi. Both the North Vietnamese and Russians immediately charged that aircraft had struck residential areas of Hanoi, killing or wounding 100 civilians. Allegedly, several foreign embassies were also hit, including Communist China's. Headquarters MACV quickly asserted that only military targets were struck. The State Department conceded that the attacking aircraft might have accidentally hit residential areas but strongly suggested that Hanoi's antiaircraft fire and SA-2 missiles (of which more than 100 were fired during the two days, a record high) may have caused the civilian damage.[7]

Debriefings of the crews of seven USAF flights participating in the 13 and 14 December strikes on the railroad yard indicated that two flights experienced problems. The crews of one had difficulty acquiring the target and were uncertain of the exact release coordinates because of clouds and a MIG attack. Although they thought the ordnance was released in the immediate target area, they conceded it might have fallen slightly southwest of a bridge located south of the railroad yard. Poor weather also prevented the crews of a second flight from seeing the railroad yard and bomb impact was not observed, although they thought the ordnance struck rolling stock.[8]

The Communist allegations -- and the growing criticism by certain groups in the United States and abroad about the war's escalation -- prompted the administration on 16 December to suspend further attacks on the Yen Vien railroad yard. On the 23d Admiral Sharp advised all subordinate commands that until further notice no air attacks were authorized within 10 nautical miles of the center of Hanoi. Attacks on other fixed targets were also halted for the time being. On 26 December a New York Times correspondent, Harrison E. Salisbury, who arrived in Hanoi on the 23d reported on alleged eyewitness accounts of the 13 and 14 December air strikes that resulted in civilian casualties and damage. The Defense Department on the same day acknowledged that some civilian areas may have been struck accidentally but reemphasized its policy to bomb only military targets in the North and to take all possible care to avoid civilian casualties. It was impossible, it said, to avoid some damage to civilian areas.[9]

Other Air Operations in November and December

Other air action in the last two months of 1966 included restrikes along the Hanoi-Lai Cai railroad line in route package V and continuation of the Tally-Ho air campaign in route package I. In fact, about 43 percent of the total U.S. air effort in the North -- and 64 percent of the USAF effort -- was directed against targets in route package I. An Air Force compilation of the results of the Tally-Ho air campaign from 20 July through November showed the following:

	Destroyed	Damaged	Other
Trucks	72	61	
Structures	1,208	624	
Watercraft	85	132	
Antiaircraft and air warning positions	92	22	
Roads cut, cratered, or seeded			339
Landslides			6
Secondary explosions			1,414

Nevertheless there was still considerable uncertainty as to the overall effect of this air program on North Vietnam's ability to resupply the South.[10]

A limited number of USAF road cutting and other air strikes were also made in route packages II, III, and IV. There were no B-52 strikes in the North in November but in December 78 sorties were flown in the DMZ and 35 sorties slightly above the zone. From 12 April 1966 when the first strike was conducted against North Vietnam through the end of the year, B-52's flew 280 sorties including 104 sorties in "DMZ North." The major B-52 effort was directed against targets in South Vietnam. Year-end operations were also highlighted by 48-hour Christmas and New Year "truces". Although bombing ceased over the North during each truce period, USAF reconnaissance flights continued. USAF attack sorties for the year totaled 44,500 -- slightly more than 54 percent of the 81,948 attack sorties flown in the North by all U.S. and VNAF aircraft.[11]

Meanwhile, the JCS in November asked Admiral Sharp to comment on the "Combat Beaver" proposal that the Air Staff had developed in conjunction with the other services to support Secretary McNamara's proposed electronic and ground barrier between North and South Vietnam. Using Steel Tiger, Gate Guard, and Tally-Ho experience, Combat Beaver called for day and night air strikes on key logistic centers. This, it was hoped, would create new concentrations of backed-up enemy materiel and equipment suitable for air strikes. It would complement any ground barrier system and could begin immediately.[12]

Admiral Sharp's comments were critical. He said that with certain exceptions Combat Beaver was similar to the current air program. He thought that it overstressed the importance of air strikes in route packages II, III, and IV and would result in high aircraft losses. It would not, in his view, increase overall air effectiveness but, instead, disrupt the existing well-balanced air effort. Taking into account CINCPAC's comments and those of other agencies, the Air Staff reworked the proposal and, at the end of December, produced a new one, designating it the integrated strike and interdiction plan (ISIP).[13]

Assessment of Enemy Air Defenses

By the end of 1966 the overwhelming number of U.S. combat aircraft losses in the North was still caused by conventional antiaircraft fire. The Seventh Air Force estimated the enemy's antiaircraft strength

CHRONOLOGY OF THE GROWTH OF NORTH VIETNAM'S AIR DEFENSES
1964-1966

Jul 64	Air defense system based on obsolescent equipment. Anti-aircraft guns, 50; SA-2's, 0; air defense radars, 24; fighter aircraft, 0.
Aug 64	Introduction of MIG-15's.
Mar 65	Introduction of improved air defense radars such as ground control intercept.
Apr 65	First use of MIG fighter aircraft. Detection of first SA-2 site under construction.
Jun 65	Increase in air defense radars to 41.
Jul 65	First SA-2 fired at U.S. aircraft. Introduction of 100mm antiaircraft guns.
Aug 65	Significant increase in low-altitude air defense radar coverage. Increase in antiaircraft strength to about 3,000 guns.
Dec 65	Introduction of MIG-21's. Beginning of emission control of air defense radar.
Mar 66	Introduction of system for identification, friend or foe.
Jul 66	First MIG use of air-to-air missiles.
Aug 66	Completion of a sophisticated air defense system. Anti-aircraft guns, 4,400; SA-2's, 20 to 25 firing battalions; air defense radars, 271; fighter aircraft, 65.
Dec 66	Air defense system includes: light and medium antiaircraft guns, 6,398; SA-2 sites, 151; SA-2 firing battalions, 25; MIG-15's and -17's, 32; MIG-21's, 15; use of air-to-air missiles.

SOURCE: Briefing Rprt on Factors Affecting A/C Losses in SEA, 26 Sep 66, prepared by Col. H.W. Hise, JCS (TS); USAF Mgt Summary (S), 6 Jan 67; p 70; Ops Review Gp, Dir/Ops, Hq USAF; N.Y. Times, Jul 66.

had grown from 5,000 to 7,400 guns during the year.* Nevertheless, U.S. aircraft losses were decreasing with 17 downed in November and 20 in December. The Air Force lost 24 -- 12 in each of the two months.[14]

The MIG threat increased in December, apparently in response to the latest U.S. attacks on important targets. During 35 encounters and 16 engagements two F-105's were lost as against one MIG. One of the losses, on 14 December, was the first one attributed to a MIG-21 air-to-air missile. Other air-to-air missiles were fired on at least five occasions during the month, but U.S. air superiority was easily maintained. Between 3 April 1965, when the MIG's first entered the war, and 31 December 1966 there were a total of 179 encounters and 93 engagements. The aerial battles cost the enemy 28 MIG's as against 9 U.S. aircraft, a ratio of 1 to 2.8. Of the nine losses, seven were USAF and two were Navy. In addition, there were two "probable" USAF losses to MIG's. In December, the enemy's combat aircraft inventory, recently augmented by Soviet deliveries, was believed to consist of 32 MIG-15's and -17's, 15 MIG-21's, and six IL-28's, all at Phuc Yen airfield.[15]

SA-2's continued to take a small but steady toll. They claimed one USAF aircraft in November and three in December. Because the missiles precluded the use of optimum air tactics, Admiral Sharp on 22 November proposed to the JCS a major effort to solve the SA-2 problem. He placed the current SA-2 strength at 28 to 32 firing battalions+ and warned that the number would increase unless air restrictions were eased. Already a shortage of special munitions and properly equipped aircraft prevented a

---

* See p 64 and app 8.

\+ The year-end estimate was 25 battalions. See p 64.

large-scale attack on these mobile, well-camouflaged units. Only a "blitzkrieg" type of attack could prevent their movement.[16]

For the short term, Admiral Sharp recommended the use of all available aircraft to detect SA-2 sites, revision of the current targeting system to include SA-2 assembly and storage areas regardless of location, a priority intelligence effort to locate key SA-2 control facilities, and attacks on high priority targets in the North in random fashion to avoid establishing a predictable pattern of attack. He also urged steps to increase Shrike production, assure positive control and tracking of all U.S. aircraft through the USAF "Big Eye" EC-121 program, improve distribution of SA-2 data, exploit more fully color photography in penetrating camouflage, and equip all aircraft with ECM, chaff, homing radars, and warning receivers. Further, the State and Defense Departments should release statements to discourage the Soviets from deploying additional SA-2 systems by pointing to the danger of escalation, and the "intelligence community" should constantly review and distribute all relevant SA-2 information.

For the long term, Admiral Sharp said there was a need to expedite procurement of an antiradiation missile, develop better warheads using the implosion principle, employ beacons to aid in finding SA-2 emitters, provide VHF/UHF homing capabilities for Wild Weasel aircraft, and improve data exchange between the Rome Air Development Center and Southeast Asia operational activities.[17]

The Air Staff generally agreed with Admiral Sharp's recommendations. The JCS also concurred and directed General McConnell to procure and deploy adequate numbers of anti-SA-2 devices and equipment. The Joint Chiefs were still undecided at the end of the year whether to recommend to Secretary McNamara an all-out campaign against the SA-2's in the immediate future.[18]

Assessments of the Air War Against North Vietnam

As 1966 ended, General McConnell and the Air Staff remained convinced that greater use of air power, especially in North Vietnam, was the only alternative to a long, costly war of attrition. They also thought it would make unnecessary the massive buildup of U.S. and allied ground forces still under way. Although the combined air and ground effort in Southeast Asia had prevented a Communist takeover of South Vietnam, one Air Staff assessment found no significant trend toward the attainment of other U.S. objectives in that country.[19]

Within the JCS General McConnell continued to support recommendations to reduce operational restrictions and expand target coverage in the North. The level of air effort was less than he desired, but he believed air power had shown how it could be tailored to the geography of a country and, by the selection of weapons and mode of air attack, be responsive to political and psychological considerations. In some instances, it was clear, the Vietnam experience ran counter to conventional air power concepts. As he had observed in May, "tactical bombing" in South Vietnam was being conducted in part by "strategic" B-52 bombers and "strategic" bombing of the North was being conducted largely by "tactical bombers".[20]

(U) Any evaluation of the effect of air power, especially in the North, had to consider political factors which limited military activity. To deal with this circumstance, General McConnell offered the following dictum: "Since air power, like our other military forces, serves a political objective, it is also subject to political restraints. Therefore, we must qualify any assessments of air power's effectiveness on the basis of limitations that govern its application."[21]

General Harris, the PACAF commander, singled out three principal factors hampering the air campaign against North Vietnam: political restraints and geographical sanctuaries that precluded striking more lucrative targets, poor weather for prolonged periods of time, and Hanoi's ability to repair and reconstruct damaged target areas. With respect to the last, PACAF officials acknowledged the North Vietnamese had "exceptional" recuperative capabilities to counter air attacks on trucks, rolling stock, and the lines of communications. They had built road and rail by-passes and bridges in minimum time, dispersed POL by using pack animals, human porters and watercraft, and developed an effective air defense system. Infiltration through the DMZ, Laos, and Cambodia was placed at 7,000 to 9,000 men per month,* and the enemy logistic system was supporting an estimated 128,000 combat and combat support personnel with out-of-country resources. General Harris thought that an important "lesson learned" was that the gradual, drawn-out air campaign had created very little psychological impact on Hanoi's leaders and the populace. He also continued to believe (as did the Air Staff and other Air Force commanders in Southeast Asia) that control of air operations in the North -- as well as in Laos and South Vietnam -- was too fragmented and should be centralized under a single air commander.[22]

Admiral Sharp's view of the air campaign against the North in 1966 was that little had been accomplished in preventing external assistance to the enemy. Except for the June strikes on POL targets in Haiphong

---

* MACV and DIA eventually estimated that about 81,000 North Vietnamese entered South Vietnam in 1966. The infiltration rate was high in the first half and dropped sharply in the second half of the year.

(which handled 85 percent of the North's imports during the year), the port was almost undisturbed. Of the nearly 82,000 attack sorties flown during the year, less than one percent were against JCS-proposed targets. In the critical northeast area (route packages VIA and VIB), of 104 targets only 19 were hit in 1965 and 20 in 1966; the remaining 99 percent of attack sorties were armed reconnaissance and flown to harass, disrupt, and impede the movement of men and supplies on thousands of miles of roads, trails, and inland and coastal waterways. He noted that despite severe losses of vehicles, rolling stock, watercraft, supplies and men from air attack, the North Vietnamese were ingenious in hiding and dispersing their supplies and showed "remarkable" recuperative ability. He concluded that the overall amount of supplies and men moving through the DMZ, Laos, and Cambodia into South Vietnam probably was greater in 1966 than in 1965.[23]

(U) Secretary Brown took a somewhat different view of the air campaign believing it had inflicted "serious" logistic losses on the North. From 2 March 1965 (when the Rolling Thunder program began) through September 1966, air strikes had destroyed or damaged more than 7,000 trucks, 3,000 railway cars, 5,000 bridges, 15,000 barges and boats, two-thirds of the POL storage capacity, and many ammunition sites and other facilities. He cited prisoner of war reports indicating that troops in the South received no more than 50 percent of daily supply requirements.[*] In addition, the air war had diverted 200,000 to 300,000 personnel to road, rail, and bridge repair work, and combat troops for air defense.[+] By December, military action in both North and South Vietnam had reduced battalion size attacks from seven

---

[*] See p 8.

[+] On 1 March 1967, Secretary McNamara estimated that Hanoi was using 125,000 men for its air defenses and "tens of thousands" of others for coastal defense.

to two per month and, in the past eight months, raised enemy casualties from 3,600 to 5,200 per month.

(U) Although infiltration from the North continued, Secretary Brown said: "I do not believe that an air blockade of land and sea routes will ever be completely effective any more than a sea blockade can prevent all commerce from entering or leaving a country." He thought the air attacks were becoming more effective due to improvements in intelligence, tactics, equipment, and techniques.

(U) The Air Force Secretary defended the administration's policy of exempting certain targets from air attack if they supported only the North's civilian economy, were close to urban areas and would cause civilian suffering if hit, and would not significantly affect in the short term the enemy's ability to continue fighting. He listed five criteria for judging whether to strike a target: its effect on infiltration from North to South, the extent of air defenses and possible U.S. aircraft losses, the degree of "penalty" inflicted on North Vietnam, the possibility of civilian casualties, and the danger of Soviet or Chinese intervention resulting in a larger war. He thought that a "Korean-type" victory -- with the aggressor pushed back and shown that aggression did not pay -- would meet U.S. objectives and make the war in Vietnam a "success." [24]

Secretary McNamara's views on the controlled use of air power against the North were well known. In a "deployment issue" paper sent to the JCS on 6 October in conjunction with deployment planning, he said that intelligence reports and aerial reconnaissance clearly showed how the air program against the North effectively harassed and delayed truck movements and materiel into the South but had no effect on troop infiltration moving along trails. He thought that the cost to the enemy to replace trucks and cargo as a result of stepped up air strikes would be negligible compared with the cost of greatly increased U.S. aircraft losses. In a summation of his views on the war before House Subcommittees in February 1967 he further stated:

> For those who thought that air attacks on North Vietnam would end the aggression in South Vietnam, the results from this phase of the operations have been disappointing. But for those who understood the political and economic structure of North Vietnam, the results have been satisfactory. Most of the war materiel sent from North Vietnam to South Vietnam is provided by other Communist countries and no amount of destruction of the industrial capacity . . . can, by itself, eliminate this flow . . . .

When the bombing campaign began he added, "we did not believe that air attacks on North Vietnam, by themselves, would bring its leaders to the conference table or break the morale of its people -- and they have not done so."

(U) The Defense Secretary also observed that although air strikes had destroyed two-thirds of their POL storage capacity, the North Vietnamese had continued to bring it in "over the beach" and disperse it. POL shortages did not appear to have greatly impeded the North's war effort. He reiterated the U.S. policy that "the bombing of the North is intended as a supplement to and not a substitute for the military operations in the South." [25]

NOTES

Chapter I

1. Hist (TS), CINCPAC, 1965, vol II, pp 326 and 328; Project CHECO SEA Rprt (TS), 15 Dec 66, subj: Comd and Control, 1965, pp 1-7; memo (TS), Lt Col B.F. Echols, Exec, Dir/Plans to AFCHO, 27 Nov 67, subj: Review of Draft Hist Study, "The Air Campaign Against NVN."

2. Hist (TS), CINCPAC, 1965, vol II, pp 326 and 328; Testimony of Gen J.P. McConnell, CSAF on 9 May 66 before Senate Preparedness Investigating Subcmte of Cmte on Armed Services, 89th Cong, 2d Sess (U) 9-10 May 66, USAF Tactical Air Ops and Readiness, pp 25-26.

3. Rprt (TS), An Eval of the Effects of the Air Campaign Against NVN and Laos, prepared by Jt Staff, Nov 66, in Dir/Plans; Talking Paper for the JCS for the State-JCS Mtg on 1 Apr 66 (TS), Undated, subj: Discussions with Mr. Bundy on Far Eastern Matters, in Dir/Plans; Hist (TS), CINCPAC, 1965, vol II, pp 339-41; memo (TS), Col D.G. Gravenstine, Chief Ops Review Gp, Dir/Ops to AFCHO, 22 Nov 67, subj: Draft of AFCHO Hist Study.

4. Memo (TS), Col J.C. Berger, Asst Dir for Jt Matters, Dir/Ops to CSAF, 10 Aug 66; Background Paper on Division of R/T Area (TS), Mar 66, both in Dir/Plans; Excerpts from Gen Moore's Presentation to the JCS (TS), 13 Jul 66, in OSAF; Project CHECO SEA Rprts (TS), 15 Dec 66, subj: Comd and Control, 1965, pp 1-9; and 1 Mar 67, subj: Control of Air Strikes in SEA, pp 95-97; memo (TS), Echols to AFCHO, 27 Nov 67.

5. Van Staaveren (TS), 1965, pp 71-74; N.Y. Times, 1 Feb 66.

6. Memo (TS), Col J.H. Germeraad, Asst Dep Dir of Plans for War Plans, Dir/Plans to CSAF, 10 Jan 66, subj: Strat for SEA; Background Paper on Pertinent Testimony by SECDEF and JCS given on 20 Jan 66 (TS), 20 Jan 66, both in Dir/Plans.

7. JCSM-16-66 (TS), 8 Jan 66.

8. Memo (TS), Lt Gen J.T. Carroll, Dir DIA to SECDEF, 21 Jan 66, subj: An Appraisal of the Bombing of NVN, in Dir/Plans; JCSM-41-66 (TS), 18 Jan 66.

9. JCSM-56-66 (TS), 25 Jan 66.

10. JCS 2343/751 (TS), 13 Jan 66; SM-82-66 (TS), 22 Jan 66.

11. Memo (TS), SECDEF to Chmn JCS, 5 Jan 66, no subj: in Dir/Plans; CM-1135-66 (TS), 22 Jan 66.

Notes to Pages 7 - 14   73

12. Testimony of Secy McNamara on 26 Jan 66 before House Subcmte on Appns, 89th Cong, 2d Sess (U), Supplemental Def Appns for 1966, p 31.

13. Ibid., p 32; background briefing by U.S. officials (U), 31 Jan 66, in SAFOI.

14. Memo (TS), SECDEF to Pres, 24 Jan 66, subj: The Mil Outlook in SVN, in Dir/Plans; Hist (TS), CINCPAC, 1966, vol II, p 605.

15. Wash Post, 1 Feb 66; N.Y. Times, 1 Feb 66.

16. Intvw (U), McConnell with Hearst Panel, 21 Mar 66, in SAFOI; Hist (TS), CINCPAC, 1966, vol II, p 491; Rprt (TS), Dir/Ops, 20 Apr 66, subj: SEA Counter-Air Alternatives, p A-28, in AFCHO.

17. Memo (TS), Col D.G. Cooper, Ofc Dep Dir of Plans for War Plans, Dir/Plans to CSAF, 12 Feb 66, subj: The Employment of Air Power in the War in NVN; Briefing of JCS R/T Study Gp Rprt (TS), 6 Apr 66, subj: Air Ops Against NVN, App A; Rprt (TS), An Eval of Effect of the Air Campaign Against NVN and Laos, all in Dir/Plans; Hist (TS), CINCPAC, 1966, vol II, pp 493-44; Jacob Van Staaveren, USAF Deployment Planning for SEA (AFCHO, 1966) (TS), pp 1-2 and 26 (hereinafter cited as Van Staaveren, 1966).

18. CM-1147-66 (TS), 1 Feb 66.

19. Hist (TS), CINCPAC, 1966, vol II, pp 510-11; Van Staaveren (TS), 1966, ch II.

20. Memo (U), Lt Gen H.T. Wheless, Asst Vice CSAF to Deps, Dirs, Chiefs of Comparable Ofces, 17 Feb 66, subj: Analysis of Air Power, in Dir/Plans; Van Staaveren, 1966, pp 10-15.

21. Memo (S), Lt Gen R.R. Compton, DCS/P&O to DCS/P&R, 21 Feb 66, subj: Organization in SEA, in Dir/Plans.

22. Memo (TS), Maj Gen S.J. McKee, Asst DCS/Plans and Ops for JCS to CSAF, 18 Feb 66, subj: Air Ops Against NVN; JCSM-113-66 (TS), 19 Feb 66, both in Dir/Plans.

23. Testimony of Secy McNamara on 25 Jan 66 before House Subcmte on Appns, 89th Cong, 2d Sess (U), Supplementary Def Appns for 1966, pp 33 and 39; memo (TS), Cooper to CSAF, 12 Feb 66, subj: The Employment of Air Power in the War in VN; memo (TS), McKee to SECDEF, 24 Mar 66, subj: Air Ops against NVN, both in Dir/Plans; N.Y. Times, 5 Feb 66.

Chapter II

1. Jacob Van Staaveren, USAF Plans and Operations in Southeast Asia (AFCHO, 1965) (TS), p 50 (hereinafter cited as Van Staaveren, 1965); Van Staaveren, 1966, pp 4 and 19.

2. Rprt (S), SEA Air Ops, Mar 66, pp 2-3, prepared by Dir/Tac Eval, Hqs PACAF (hereinafter cited as PACAF rprt); JCS R/T Study Gp Rprt (TS), 6 Apr 67, App A; ltr (TS), CINCPAC to JCS, 18 Sep, subj: An Eval of CY 66-67 Force Rqmts; rprt (TS), Eval of Effects of the Air Campaign Against NVN and Laos, Nov 66, all in Dir/Plans; JCSM-153-66 (TS), 10 Mar 66.

3. Memo (TS), McKee to Gen. W. H. Blanchard, Vice CSAF, 23 Mar 66, subj: Air Ops Against Aflds in NVN, in Dir/Ops; Hist (TS) MACV, 1966, p 431; Hist (TS), CINCPAC, 1966, Vol II, p 494.

4. Memo (TS), McKee to CSAF, 25 Mar 66, subj: Acft Losses Over NVN, w/atch Talking Paper, in Dir/Plans; intvw (U), McConnell with Hearst Panel, 21 Mar 66 in SAFOI; rprt (TS), Dir/Plans, 20 Apr 66, p A-34; N.Y. Journal American, 20 Mar 66.

5. Hist (S), Dir/Ops, Jul-Dec 66, p 10; Hq USAF Ops Analysis Initial Progress Rprt (S), Mar 66, subj: Analysis of Effectiveness of Interdiction in SEA, in AFCHO.

6. Hq USAF Ops Analysis Second Progress Rprt (S), May 66, subj: Analysis of Effectiveness of Air Interdiction in SEA, ch V, in AFCHO.

7. Summary of Action by JCS (TS), 25 Mar 66, subj: Air Ops Against NVN, in Dir/Plans; Hist (TS), CINCPAC, 1966, vol II, p 497.

8. CSAFM-W-66 (TS), 20 Jan 66; CSAFM-P-23-66 and CMCM-33-66 (TS), 18 Apr 66; Talking Paper on Air Interdiction NVN/Laos (TS), 6 Jul 66; rprt (TS), An Eval of the Effects of the Air Campaign Against NVN and Laos, Nov 66, all in Dir/Plans; Hist (TS), CINCPAC, 1966, vol II, p 497; Hist (TS), MACV 1966, p 431.

9. CSAFM-W-66 (TS), 20 Jun 66; rprt (TS), An Eval of the Effects of the Air Campaign Against NVN and Laos, Nov 66, PACAF rprt (S), SEA Air Ops, Apr 66, pp 3-8, all in Dir/Plans.

10. DAF Order No 559N (U), 26 Mar 66, in AFCHO; Hist (TS), CINCPAC, 1966, vol II, p 468; tel to Ofc of Asst for Gen Officer Matters, DCS/P (U), 15 Aug 67.

11. PACAF rprt (S), SEA Air Ops, Apr 66, p 388, in Dir/Ops; Seventh AF Chronology, 1 Jul 65-30 Jun 66 (S), p 48; Hq USAF Ops Analysis Second Progress Rprt (S), May 66, pp 39-44, both in AFCHO; Project CHECO SEA Rprts (TS), 15 Jul 67, subj: R/T, Jul 65-Dec 66, p 50, and 21 Jul 67, subj: Expansion of USAF Ops in SEA, 1966, pp 100-03; Hist (TS), CINCPAC, 1966, vol II, p 575.

12. Seventh AF Chronology, 1 Jul 65-30 Jun 66, p 51; PACAF rprt (S), SEA Air Ops, Apr 66, pp 3-8.

13. Background Paper on the Division of the R/T Area (TS), Mar 66; Talking Paper on the Division of the R/T Area (TS), Mar 66, both in Dir/Plans; Hist (TS), CINCPAC, 1966, vol II, pp 494-95.

14. Memo (TS), McKee to CSAF, 16 Apr 66, subj: Priority of Air Effort in SEA; memo (TS), SECDEF to Chmn JCS, 14 Apr 66, no subj: ltr (TS), CINCPAC to JCS, 18 Sep 66, subj: Eval of CY 66-67 Force Rqmts w/atch MACV Rprt (TS), 5 Sep 66; CM-1354-66 (TS), 20 Apr 66; Background Paper on R/T Areas (TS), Mar 66, all in Dir/Plans; Hist (TS), CINCPAC, 1966, vol II, pp 494-97; memo (TS), Gravenstine to AFCHO, 22 Nov 67.

15. JCS 2343/805-1 (TS), 14 Apr 66.

16. CSAFM-P-30-66 (TS), 20 Apr 66; memo (TS), Maj Gen L. D. Clay, Dep Dir of Plans to CSAF, 26 Jul 66, subj: U.S. Strat for SEA and S.W. Pacific; JCS 2343/805-1 (TS), 14 Apr 66; JCS 2343/805-5, 22 Jul 66, all in Dir/Plans.

17. JCS R/T Study Gp Rprt (TS), 6 Apr 66, subj: Air Ops Against NVN; memo (TS), McKee to CSAF, 13 Apr 66, subj: R/T Study Gp Rprt, Air Ops Against NVN; memo (TS), Gravenstine to AFCHO, 22 Nov 66.

18. CSAFM-P-22-66 (TS), 13 Apr 66; memo (TS), McKee to CSAF, 13 Apr 66; JCSM-238-66 (TS), 14 Apr 66, all in Dir/Plans.

19. Transcript (U), Secy Brown's remarks on "Meet the Press," 22 May 66, in SAFOI.

20. Memo (S), Berger to CSAF, 15 Sep 66, subj: 7th AF Ops in RP II, III, and IV; PACAF rprt (S), SEA Air Ops, May 66, pp 1-8, both in Dir/Plans.

21. PACAF rprt (S), SEA Air Ops, May 66, pp 1-8; Seventh AF Chronology, 1 Jul 65 to 30 Jun 66, p 52; ltr (TS), CINCPAC to JCS, 18 Sep 66; Project CHECO SEA Rprts (TS), 9 Sep 66, subj: Night Interdiction in SEA, pp 33-37, and 25 May 67, subj: Interdiction in SEA (1965-1966), pp 39-69.

22. Testimony of McConnell on 9 May 66 before Senate Preparedness Investigating Subcmte (TS), pp 16-17 (AFCHO's classified copy); PACAF rprt (S), SEA Air Ops, May 66, pp 1-8 and 22; CINCPACFLT Analysis Staff Study 9-66 (TS), 12 Jul 66, subj: Combat Effectiveness of the SA-2 through Mid-1966, both in Dir/Plans.

23. Memo (S), Maj Gen R. N. Smith, Dir of Plans to DCS/P&O, 3 May 66, subj: Capabilities for Aerial Blockade; msg 87716 (TS), CSAF to SAC, PACAF, TAC, USAFE, 6 May 66, both in Dir/Plans.

24. Msg 95413 (TS), CINCPACAF to CSAF, 24 May 66, in Dir/Plans.

25. Hist (S), Dir/Ops, Jul-Dec 66, p 126; PACAF rprt (S), SEA Air Ops, Jun 66, pp 6-9; Seventh AF Chronology, 1 Jul 65-30 Jun 66, (S), p 52; ltr (TS), CINCPAC to JCS, 18 Sep 66; Project CHECO SEA Rprt (S), 9 Aug 67, subj: Combat Skyspot, pp 6 and 19; Project CHECO SEA Rprt (TS), 9 Sep 66, subj: Night Interdiction in SEA, pp 33-37.

26. PACAF rprt (S), SEA Air Ops, Jun 66, pp 6-9; Project CHECO SEA Rprt (TS), 9 Sep 66, subj: Night Interdiction in SEA, pp 33-37.

27. Project CHECO SEA Rprt (TS), 25 May 67, subj: Interdiction in SEA, 1965-1966, pp 60-61.

Chapter III

1. Memo (TS), R. Helms, Acting Dir CIA to Dep SECDEF, 27 Dec 65, subj: Probable Reaction to U.S. Bombing of POL Targets in NVN, in Dir/Plans.

2. Memo (TS), McKee to SECDEF, 24 Mar 66, subj: Air Ops Against NVN; memo (S), C.R. Vance, Dep SECDEF to Chmn JCS, 25 Apr 66, same subj; memo (TS), W.W. Rostow, Spec Asst to Pres to Secys State and Def, 6 May 66, no subj, all in Dir/Plans; study (TS), 27 Oct 66, subj: Effectiveness of Air Strikes Against NVN, prepared by Sys Analysis Div, Dept of Navy, in OSAF.

3. Memo (TS), Smith to CSAF, 16 Jun 66, subj: NVN Strike Prog, in Dir/Plans; Hist (TS), CINCPAC, 1966, vol II, p 498.

4. Ibid.; Testimony of McConnell on 9 May 66 before Senate Preparedness Investigating Subcmte of the Cmte on Armed Services (U), p 27.

5. Project CHECO SEA Rprt (TS), 15 Jul 67, subj: R/T, Jul 65-Dec 66, p 59; N.Y. News, 24 Jun 66; Wash Post, 30 Jun 66, N.Y. Times, 1 Jul 66.

6. Hist (TS), CINCPAC, 1966, vol II, pp 499-500; Hist (TS), MACV 1966, p 431; Wash Post, 26 Jun 66; Balt Sun, 27 Jun 66.

7. Project CHECO SEA Rprt (TS), 15 Jul 67, subj: R/T, Jul 65-Dec 66, p 64; Hist (TS), CINCPAC, 1966, vol II, pp 499-500; Van Staaveren, 1966, p 42; N.Y. Times, 1 Jul 66.

8. Wash Post, 30 Jun 66.

9. N.Y. Times, 1 Jul 66; Van Staaveren, 1966, p 42.

10. Ltr (TS), CINCPAC to JCS, 4 Aug 66, subj: CINCPAC Briefing for SECDEF, 8 Jul 66; memo (TS), A. Enthoven, Asst SECDEF for Sys Analysis to Secys of Mil Depts et al, 12 Jul 66, subj: CINCPAC July 8, 1966 Briefing, both in Dir/Plans; Hist (TS), CINCPAC, 1966, vol II, pp 510-11.

11. Ltr (TS), CINCPAC to JCS, 4 Aug 66; memo (TS), Enthoven to Secys of Mil Depts et al, 12 Jul 66.

12. Van Staaveren, 1966, pp 42-53.

Notes to Pages 35 - 40   77

13. PACAF rprt (S), SEA Air Ops, Jul 66, pp 4-7; Rpt (TS), An Eval of the Effect of the Air Campaign Against NVN and Laos, Nov 66; ltr (TS), CINCPAC to JCS, 4 Aug 66.

14. Hist (S), Dir/Ops, Jul-Dec 66, pp 13 and 20-22.

15. Memo (TS), Berger to CSAF, 15 Sep 66; Excerpts from Gen Moore's Presentation to the JCS (TS), 13 Jul 66; PACAF rprt (S), SEA Air Ops, Jul 66, pp 4-7; memo (TS), Gravenstine to AFCHO, 22 Nov 67.

16. Talking Paper for JCS for Their Mtg with Adm Sharp at the JCS Mtg of 23 Sep 66 (TS), 22 Sep 66, in Dir/Plans; PACAF rprt (S), SEA Air Ops, Aug 66, pp 1-2; Hist (TS), CINCPAC, 1966, vol II, pp 500-02.

17. Memo (TS), M/Gen J.E. Thomas, Asst CS/I to SAF, 14 Oct 66, subj: PACAF Rprt on the NVN POL Situation, in Dir/Plans.

18. PACAF Rprts (S), SEA Air Ops, Jul 66, pp 4-5, Aug 66, pp 1-3; Sep 66, pp 4 and 8; and Oct 66, pp 10-11, all in Ops Review Gp, Dir/Ops.

19. Talking Paper for JCS for Their Mtg with Adm Sharp . . . on 23 Sep 66 (TS), 22 Sep 66; PACAF rprts (S), SEA Air Ops, Jul 66, pp 4-5 and 20; Aug 66, p 22; Sep 66, p 23; and Oct 66, p 23.

20. PACAF rprt (S), SEA Air Ops, Jul 66, pp 4-5 and 20; N.Y. Times, 8 Jul 66 and 9 Aug 66; Wash Star, 8 Aug 66; Balt Sun, 22 Sep 66.

21. Project CHECO SEA Rprt (TS), 9 Sep 66, subj: Night Interdiction in SEA, pp 37-38; ltr (TS), CINCPAC to JCS, 18 Sep 66; Hist (TS), MACV, 1966, p 434; N.Y. Times, 31 Jul 66.

22. Project CHECO SEA Rpts (TS), 9 Sep 66, subj: Night Interdiction in SEA, pp 37-38; 21 Nov 66, subj: Operation Tally-Ho, pp vi and 1-12; 15 Feb 67, subj: Air Ops in the DMZ Area, pp 35-42; and 15 May 67, subj: Air Interdiction in SEA, pp 61 and 64; briefing (TS), by Brig Gen C.M. Talbott, Dep Dir Tac Air Control Center, 7th AF for SECDEF et al (Saigon), 10 Oct 66, Doc No 13 in Project CHECO SEA Rprt, 15 Feb 67 pt II; PACAF rprt (S), SEA Air Ops, Jul 66, pp 7-8; Wash Star, 1 Aug 66.

23. Memo (TS), Rear Adm F.J. Bloui, Dir Fast East Region, OSD to Dir of Jt Staff, 1 Jun 66, subj: Air Ops in the DMZ; msg (TS), JCS to CINCPAC, 20 Jun 66, both in Dir/Plans; Hist (TS), MACV, 1966, pp 24-25.

24. PACAF rprt (S), SEA Air Ops, Aug 66, p 6; JCSM-603-66 (TS), 17 Sep 66; N.Y. Times, 31 Jul 66.

25. Memo (S), McConnell to Dep SECDEF, 25 Aug 66, no subj, in Dir/Plans; Hist (S), Dir/Ops, Jul 66, p 255; Project CHECO SEA Rprt (TS), 21 Nov 66, subj: Operation Tally-Ho, pp 17-25.

26. PACAF rprt (S), SEA Air Ops, Oct 66, p 2; Project CHECO SEA Rprt (TS), 15 Feb 67, subj: Air Ops in the DMZ area, pp 22, 26-28, 37, and 41.

27. Project CHECO SEA Rprt (TS), 25 May 67, subj: Air Interdiction in SEA, 1965-1966, pp 64-65.

28. Memo for record (S), by Lt Col L. F. Duggan, Exec Asst Ofc, Dir Jt Staff, 13 Oct 66, no subj; memo (TS), undated, subj: JCS Assessment of the Threat, both in Dir/Plans; Briefing (TS), by Brig Gen Talbott, 10 Oct 66; Project CHECO SEA Rprt (TS), 15 Feb 67, subj: Air Ops in the DMZ area, 1966, pp 24-25 and 51; PACAF rprt (S), SEA Air Ops, pp 1-7 and 17.

29. Memo (TS), Holloway to SAF, 19 Oct 66, subj: Results of Air Effort Upon Movement Through NVN/SVN DMZ During Aug 66, in Dir/Plans.

30. Project CHECO SEA Rprt (TS), 25 May 67, subj: Air Interdiction in SEA, 1965-1966, p 68; Doc 96 in Project CHECO SEA Rprt, 15 Feb 67, pt II.

Chapter IV

1. Hist (S), Dir/Ops, Jul-Dec 66, pp 20-23.

2. Memo (S), Col F.W. Vetter, Mil Asst to SAF to Vice CSAF, 3 Aug 66, subj: Significance of Watercraft Destroyed in NVN, in Dir/Plans.

3. Ibid.

4. Hist (S), Dir/Ops, Jul-Dec 66, pp 23-24; memo (TS), Gravenstine to AFCHO, 22 Nov 66.

5. Memo (TS), SECDEF to SAF, SN, 2 Sep 66, subj: Night Ops in SEA, in OSAF.

6. Ibid.

7. Memo (S), SN to SECDEF, 28 Sep 66, subj: Study Results: Night Ops in NVN, in OSAF.

8. Memo (S), SAF to SECDEF, 10 Nov 66, no subj; study (TS), 27 Oct 66, subj: Effectiveness of Air Strikes Against NVN.

9. Memo (TS), SN to SECDEF, 3 Nov 66, subj: Study of Effectiveness of Air Strikes Against NVN w/atch study (TS), 27 Oct 67, subj: Effectiveness of Air Strikes, both in OSAF; memo (TS), Gravenstine to AFCHO, 22 Nov 67.

10. Memo (TS), SAF to SECDEF, 10 Nov 66.

Notes to Pages 49 - 58

11. Memo (S), SAF to SECDEF, 19 Jul 66, subj: A/C Attrition in SEA, in Dir/Plans.

12. Ibid.

13. Memo (S), SAF to SECDEF, 24 Aug 66, subj: Questions Resulting from Briefing on Night Ops in SEA; memo (TS), McConnell to Dep SECDEF, 25 Aug 66, subj: JCS 2343/894-1, 25 Aug 66, both in OSAF.

14. Memo (S), Clay to CSAF, 25 Aug 66, subj: SEA Tac Ftr Attrition and A/C Proc Prog; memo (S), Holloway to Chmn JCS, 29 Aug 66, subj: SEA Tac Ftr Attrition and A/C Procur, both in Dir/Plans.

15. N.Y. Times, 23 Sep 66.

16. Briefing Rprt of Factors Affecting A/C Losses in SEA (S), 26 Sep 66, prepared by Col. H.W. Hise, Chmn, JCS A/C Losses Study Gp; JCS A/C Losses Study Gp Rprt (TS), Nov 66, subj: Factors Affecting Combat Air Ops and A/C Losses in SEA, both in Dir/Plans.

17. Msg 20135 (S), CINCPACAF to CSAF, 20 Oct 66, in OSAF; CINCPACFLT Analysis Staff Study 9-66 (TS), 12 Jul 66, subj: Combat Effectiveness of the SA-2 Through Mid-1966; Briefing Rprt of Factors Affecting A/C Losses in SEA (S), 26 Sep 66, both in Dir/Plans; Hist (S), Dir/Ops, Jul-Dec 66, pp 272-74.

18. Msg 20135 (S), CINCPACAF to CSAF, 20 Oct 66; Briefing Rprt of Factors Affecting A/C Losses in SEA (S), 26 Sep 66.

19. Memos (S), Clay to CSAF, 23 and 27 Sep and 3 Oct 66, same subjs: Factors Affecting A/C Losses in SEA, in Dir/Plans; JCSM-651-66, 10 Oct 66.

20. Memo (U), 22 Oct 66, subj: Secy Brown's Questions Concerning the Hise Rprt, in OSAF; Talking Paper for Chmn JCS on an Analysis of Air Ops in NVN to be discussed with SECDEF on 12 Nov 66 (TS), 11 Nov 66, subj: Analysis of Air Ops in NVN, both in Dir/Plans; JCS 2343/956-1 (TS), 15 Nov 66.

21. Memo (S), SECDEF to Chmn JCS, 17 Sep 66, subj: SEA Utilization of A/C, in OSAF; transcript (U), SECDEF News Briefing, 22 Sep 66, in SAFOI.

22. Memo (TS), Chief, PAC Div, Jt Staff to J-3, 17 Sep 66, subj: Utilization of A/C in SEA; in OSAF; JCSM-646-66 (TS), 6 Oct 66.

23. JCSM-645-66 (TS), 6 Oct 66; JCSM-646-66, 6 Oct 66.

Chapter V

1. Van Staaveren, 1966, ch V.

2. CM-1906-66 (TS), 8 Nov 66; memo (TS), Gravenstine to AFCHO, 22 Nov 67.

3. Memo (TS), SAF to SECDEF, 10 Nov 66, no subj, w/atch Interim Reply on Air Staff Action Items Resulting from SECDEF Trip to SEA, 10-14 Oct 66, in OSAF.

4. PACAF rprt (S), SEA Air Ops, Nov 66, pp 1-4; rprt (TS), An Eval of the Effects of the Air Campaign on NVN and Laos, Nov 66, both in Dir/Plans; Van Staaveren, 1966, pp 63-66.

5. PACAF rprts (S), SEA Air Ops, Nov 66, pp 1-9; Dec 66, pp 1-8, both in Dir/Plans.

6. Ibid.; Project CHECO SEA Rprt (TS), 15 Jul 67, subj: R/T, Jul 65-Dec 66, pp 98-99; Hist (TS), CINCPAC, 1966, vol II, pp 504-05 and 512; Balt Sun 18 Dec 66; N.Y. Times, 16 Dec 66.

7. Balt Sun, 14 Dec 66; N.Y. Times, 15 Dec 66; Wash Post, 15 and 16 Dec 66.

8. Project CHECO SEA Rprt (TS), 15 Jul 67, subj: R/T, Jul 65-Dec 66, pp 99-100.

9. Ibid.; N.Y. Times, 27 Dec 66.

10. Project CHECO SEA Rprt (TS), 25 May 67, subj: Air Interdiction in SEA, 1965-1966, p 68; PACAF rprt (S), SEA Air Ops, Nov 66, pp 1-9; Dec 66, pp 1-8.

11. Ibid.; app 1 and 2; N.Y. Times, 26, 27 Dec 66, and 3 Jan 67.

12. CASFM-D-25-66 (TS), 23 Nov 66; memo (TS), Brig Gen E.A. McDonald, Dep Dir of Plans for War Plans to Dir/Plans, 16 Dec 66, subj: Combat Beaver, both in Dir/Plans; Hist (S), Dir/Ops, Jul-Dec 66, pp 2-3 and 254.

13. Memo (TS), McDonald to Dir/Plans, 23 Nov 66; Hist (S), Dir/Ops, Jul-Dec 66, pp 2-3; Project CHECO SEA Rprt (TS), 15 Jul 67, subj: R/T, Jul 65-Dec 66, pp 94-95.

14. Project CHECO SEA Rprt (TS), 21 Jul 67, subj: Expansion of USAF Ops in SEA, 1966, p 111; PACAF rprts (S), SEA Air Ops, Nov 66, p 22; and Dec 66, p 25.

15. PACAF Chronology, Jul 65-Jun 66 (S), in AFCHO; PACAF rprts (S), SEA Air Ops, Nov 66, pp 1-9; Dec 66, pp 1-8; Project CHECO SEA Rprt (TS), 15 Jul 67, subj: R/T, Jul 65-Dec 66, p 118; USAF Mgt Summary (S), 6 Jan 67, p 70; Hist (TS), CINCPAC, 1966, vol II, pp 522-23; app 10 and 11.

16. Ltr (TS), CINCPAC to JCS, 22 Nov 66, subj: SA-Threat Conf Rpt, in Dir/Plans; Hist (TS), CINCPAC, 1966, vol II, pp 516-19.

Notes to Pages 66 - 71

17. Ltr (TS), CINCPAC to JCS, 22 Nov 66; JCS 2343/977 (TS), 16 Dec 66.

18. Memo (TS), Col E. T. Burnett, Dep Chief, Tac Div, Dir/Ops to Asst Dir of Plans for Jt and NSC Matters, 28 Nov 66, subj: Major Recommendations of the SA-2 Conf, in Dir/Plans; JCS 2343/977 (TS), 16 Dec 66; Hist (TS), CINCPAC, 1966, vol II, p 519.

19. Van Staaveren, 1966, pp 71-74.

20. Address (U), Gen McConnell before Jt Activities Briefing, Hq USAF, 23 Nov 66, in SAFOI; Testimony of McConnell on 9 May 66 before Senate Investigating Preparedness Subcmte (U), p 29; Van Staaveren, 1966, pp 71-74.

21. Address (U), Gen McConnell before the Houston, Texas Forum, 29 Nov 66, in SAFOI.

22. Project CHECO SEA Rprts (TS), 1 Mar 67, subj: Control of Air Strikes in SEA, pp 81-99; and 23 Oct 67, subj: The War in VN, pp 44-45; memo (TS), SAF to SECDEF, 3 Jun 67, subj: Possible Course of Action in SEA; memo (TS), SAF to SECDEF, 9 Jun 67, no subj, both in Dir/Plans; memo (TS), Echols to AFCHO, 27 Nov 67.

23. Hist (TS), CINCPAC, 1966, vol II, pp 510-12 and 606-07.

24. Address (U), Secy Brown before Aviation/Space Writers Assoc Mtg, Wash D.C., 8 Dec 66, in SAFOI; Balt Sun, 9 Dec 66; rprt (U), Selected Statements on VN by DOD and Other Admin Officials, 1 Jan-30 Jun 67, p 33, in SAFOI.

25. Testimony of Secy McNamara on 20 Feb 67 before House Subcmtes of the Cmte on Appns, 90th Cong, 1st Sess, Supplemental Def Appns for 1967. p 21; Van Staaveren, 1966 pp 48-50.

APPENDIX 1

U.S. and VNAF Attack Sorties in Southeast Asia

1966

	USAF	USN	USMC	VNAF	Total
North Vietnam	44,500	32,955	3,694	799	81,948
Laos	32,115	9,044	3,601	0	44,760
South Vietnam	70,367	21,729	37,610	32,033	161,739
TOTAL	146,982	63,728	44,905	32,832	288,447

SOURCE: Annual Supplement to Summary Air Ops, SEA, CY 1966, prepared by Dir/Tac Eval, Hqs PACAF, 23 Jan 67; Ops Review Gp, Dir/Ops, Hq USAF.

APPENDIX 2

B-52 Sorties in Southeast Asia

1966

						Total
North Vietnam	176	South Vietnam	4,112	Laos	647	4,935
DMZ North	104	DMZ South	178			282
TOTAL	280		4,290		647	5,217

SOURCE: Strat Ops Div, J-3, JCS; Ops Review Gp, Dir/Ops, Hq USAF

APPENDIX 3

U.S. and VNAF Attack Sorties in North Vietnam

1966
(by Month)

	USAF	USN	USMC	VNAF	Total
Jan*	57	80	0	0	137
Feb	1,547	1,265	0	0	2,812
Mar	2,559	1,919	0	0	4,478
Apr	2,477	2,818	8	144	5,447
May	1,794	2,568	0	103	4,465
Jun	4,442	3,078	2	266	7,788
Jul	6,170	3,416	370	243	10,199
Aug	6,336	4,683+	792	21	11,832
Sep	6,376	4,953	825	6	12,160
Oct	4,932	3,147	559	4	8,642
Nov	3,681	2,938	633	8	7,260
Dec	4,129	2,090	513	4	6,736
TOTAL	44,500	32,955	3,702	799	81,956

* Bombing of North Vietnam resumed on 31 January 1966.
+ Reflects an increase from two to three aircraft carriers at "Yankee Station" beginning in August 1966.

SOURCE: Annual Supplement to Summary of Air Ops SEA, CY 1966. Prepared by Dir/Tac Eval, Hqs PACAF, 23 Jan 67; Ops Review Gp, Dir/Ops, Hq USAF.

APPENDIX 4

U.S. Aircraft Losses in Southeast Asia[*]

Hostile Causes

1965

	North Vietnam	Laos	South Vietnam	Total
USAF	82	11	64	157
USN[+]	85	8	6	99
USMC[+]	3	3	0	6
TOTAL	170	22	70	262

1966

	North Vietnam	Laos	South Vietnam	Total
USAF	172	48	76	296
USN[+]	109	7	6	122
USMC[+]	4	5	14	33
TOTAL	285	60	96	451

Operational Causes

	1965	1966	Total
USAF	64	78	142
USN[+]	27	40	67
USMC[+]	10	12	22
TOTAL	101	130	231

---

[*] Excludes helicopters. Includes losses due to enemy mortar attacks.
[+] USN and USMC figures subject to variations contingent on bookkeeping procedures.

SOURCE: Ops Review Gp, Dir/Ops, Hq USAF.

APPENDIX 5

USAF Combat Attrition in North Vietnam

1965*

Type of Sorties +	Sorties	Losses	Rate per 1,000 Sorties
Attack	11,599	63	5.43
CAP/Escort	5,675	7	1.23
Reconnaissance	3,294	9	2.73
Other	4,983	3	0.60
TOTAL	25,551	82	3.21

1966

Type of Sorties	Sorties	Losses	Rate per 1,000 Sorties
Attack	44,482	138	3.10
CAP/Escort	9,041	6	0.66
Reconnaissance	7,910	19	2.40
Other	16,587	9	0.54
TOTAL	78,020	172	2.20

* Bombing of North Vietnam began on 7 February 1965.
+ Excludes B-52 strikes.

SOURCE: Ops Review Gp, Dir/Ops, Hq USAF.

APPENDIX 6

U.S. Aircraft Losses to SA-2's

Date	Missiles Fired	Confirmed Losses			Probable Losses			Percent Confir'd	Effective Total
		USAF	USN	USMC	USAF	USN	USMC		
1965*	180	5	5	0	0	1	0	5.6	6.1
1966	1,057	13	7	0	5	6	0	1.9	2.9
TOTAL	1,237	18	12	0	5	7	0	2.4	3.4

* The first SA-2 firings were sighted in July 1965.

SOURCE: Ops Review Gp, Dir/Ops, Hq USAF.

APPENDIX 7

SA-2 Sites in North Vietnam

	Jan	Mar	Jun*	Sep	Dec
1965	0	0	4	23	64
1966	64	100	115	144	151

* The first SA-2 site was detected in April 1965.

SOURCE: Ops Review Gp, Dir/Ops, Hq USAF.

APPENDIX 8

Light and Medium Antiaircraft Artillery Guns in North Vietnam

	Jan	Feb*	Mar	Jun	Sep	Dec
1965	--	1,156	1,418	1,643	2,636	2,551
1966	2,884	3,092	3,159	4,123	5,009	6,398

* Bombing of North Vietnam began on 7 February 1965.

SOURCE: Ops Review Gp, Dir/Ops, Hq USAF.

APPENDIX 9

U.S. Aircraft Losses in Aerial Combat

	USAF	USN	USMC	Total
1965	2*	0	0	2
1966	5+	4++	0	9
TOTAL	7	4	0	11

* Consisted of 2 F-105's.
+ Consisted of 3 F-105's, 1 F-4C, 1 RC-47 and two "probables", 1 F-4C and 1 A-1.
++ Consisted of 3 F8's and 1 KA3. No "probables."

SOURCE: Ops Review Gp, Dir/Ops, Hq USAF.

APPENDIX 10

North Vietnamese Aircraft Losses in Aerial Combat

	MIG-15's	MIG-17's	MIG-21's	Total*
Destroyed by:		1965		
USAF	0	2	0	2
USN	0	3	0	3
USMC	0	0	0	0
TOTAL	0	5	0	5
		1966		
USAF	0	12	5	17
USN	0	4	2	6
USMC	0	0	0	0
TOTAL	0	16	7	23

* No "probables" listed.

SOURCE: Ops Review Gp, Dir/Ops, Hq USAF.

GLOSSARY

AB	Air Base
A/C	Aircraft
AFCHO	USAF Historical Division Liaison Office
Aflds	Airfields
Appns	Appropriations
Asst CS/	Assistant Chief of Staff, Intelligence
Atchd	Attached
CAP	Combat Air Patrol
CHECO	Contemporary Historical Evaluation of Counterinsurgency
CIA	Central Intelligence Agency
CINCPAC	Commander-in-Chief, Pacific
CM	Chairman's Memo
CMCM	Commandant Marine Corps Memo
CNO	Chief of Naval Operations
Comd	Command
COMUSM	Commander, U.S. Military Command, Vietnam
Conf	Conference
CSAFM	Chief of Staff Air Force Memo
CY	Calendar Year
DAF	Department of the Air Force
Dam	Damage
DCS/P&O	Deputy Chief of Staff, Plans and Operations
DCS/P&R	Deputy Chief of Staff, Programs and Resources
Dep	Deputy
Des	Destroyed
DIA	Defense Intelligence Agency
Dir	Director, Directorate
Dir/Ops	Directorate of Operations
Dir/Plan	Directorate of Plans
DMZ	Demilitarized Zone
DOD	Department of Defense
ECM	Electronic Countermeasure
Eval	Evaluation
FAC	Forward Air Controller
Ftr	Fighter
Gp	Group
Hist	History
ICC	International Control Commission
Intvw	Interview
JCS	Joint Chiefs of Staff
JCSM	Joint Chiefs of Staff Memo
Jt	Joint

Lat	Latitude
LOC	Lines of Communication
Long	Longitude
MACV	Military Assistance Command
Mgt	Management
Mil	Military
NSC	National Security Council
NVN	North Vietnam
Ops	Operations
OSD	Office, Secretary of Defense
OSAF	Office, Secretary of the Air Force
Pac	Pacific
PACAF	Pacific Air Forces
POL	Petroleum Oil and Lubricants
Pres	President
Prog	Program
RP	Route Package
Rprt	Report
R/T	Rolling Thunder
Rqmts	Requirements
SA	Systems Analysis
SAC	Strategic Air Command
SAF	Secretary of the Air Force
SAFOI	Secretary of the Air Force Office of Information
SECDEF	Secretary of Defense
Secy	Secretary
SM	Secretary's Memo
SN	Secretary of the Navy
SOD	Secretary of Defense
Strat	Strategic
SVN	South Vietnam
Sys	Systems
Tac	Tactical
TFS	Tactical Fighter Squadron
USAFE	United States Air Force, Europe
VC	Viet Cong
VN	Vietnam
VNAF	Vietnamese Air Force

DISTRIBUTION

HQ USAF

1. SAF-OS
2. SAF-US
3. SAF-FM
4. SAF-RD
5. SAF-IL
6. SAF-GC
7. SAF-LL
8. SAF-OI
9. SAF-OIX
10. SAF-AAR
11. AFCSA
12. AFCSAMI
13. AFCVC
14. AFCVS
15. AFBSA
16. AFGOA
17. AFIIS
18. AFJAG
19. AFNIN
20. AFADS
21. AFAMA
22. AFOAP
23. AFOAPB
24. AFOAPD
25. AFOAPG
26. AFOCC
27. AFPMC
28. AFRDC
29. AFRDC-D
30. AFRDD
31. AFRDDH
32. AFRDQ
33. AFRDQR
34. AFRRP
35. AFSLP
36. AFSME
37. AFSMS
38. AFSPD
39. AFSSS
40. AFXDC
41. AFXDO
42. AFXOP
43. AFXOPA
44-45. AFXOPG
46-47. AFXOS
48. AFXOX
49. AFXPD
50. AFXPDW
51. AFXPDWC
52. AFXPDWF
53. AFXPDWW
54. AFXPDO
55. AFXPDIP
56. AFXPDP
57. AFXPDR

MAJOR COMMANDS

58. AAC
59. ADC
60. AFCS
61. AFLC
62. AFSC
63. CAC
64. MAC
65-67. PACAF
68-69. SAC
70-71. TAC
72. USAFSO
73. USAFSS

OTHER

74-75. RAND
76-78. ASI(ASHAF-A)
79-100. AFCHO (Stock)

AFCHO PUBLICATIONS

Below is a list of AFCHO historical monographs dealing with various aspects of the conflict in Southeast Asia which may be obtained on loan or for permanent retention. Copies may be obtained by calling Oxford 6-6565 or by forwarding a written request.

USAF Counterinsurgency Doctrines and Capabilities, 1961-1962. (S-Noforn)

USAF Special Air Warfare Doctrines and Capabilities, 1963. (S-Noforn)

USAF Plans and Policies in South Vietnam, 1961-1963. (TS-Noforn)

USAF Plans and Policies in South Vietnam and Laos, 1964. (TS-Noforn)

USAF Plans and Operations in Southeast Asia, 1965. (TS-Noforn)

USAF Logistic Plans and Policies in Southeast Asia, 1965. (TS-Noforn)

USAF Logistic Plans and Policies in Southeast Asia, 1965. (TS-Noforn)

USAF Deployment Planning For Southeast Asia, 1966. (TS-Noforn)

In addition to the above monographs, there are a large number of historical studies dealing with Vietnam operations prepared by Project CHECO and by the various participating and supporting commands, including organizational histories down to the wing and squadron level.

USAF PLANS AND OPERATIONS

THE AIR CAMPAIGN AGAINST NORTH VIETNAM

1966

(U)

by

Jacob Van Staaveren

USAF Historical Division Liaison Office

January 1968

When this Study is no longer needed, please return it to the USAF Historical Division Liaison Office.

FOREWORD

<u>USAF Plans and Operations: The Air Campaign Against North Vietnam, 1966</u>, is the seventh of a series of historical studies on the war in Southeast Asia prepared by the USAF Historical Division Liaison Office. The previous monographs covered plans, policies, and operations in the theater beginning in 1961.

The current history reviews the political background and top level discussions leading to the renewed bombing campaign in early 1966, the restrictions still imposed on air operations, and the positions taken on them by the military chiefs. It discusses the various studies and events which led to the President's decision to strike at North Vietnam's oil storage facilities and the results of those mid-year attacks. It also examines the increasing effectiveness of enemy air defenses and the continuing assessments of the air campaign under way at year's end.

MAX ROSENBERG
Chief
USAF Historical Division
  Liaison Office

NOTE

Listed below are the code names of certain air concepts, operations, programs, and aircraft cited in this study. The reader may find it helpful to refer to the list on occasion.

Barrel Roll — Initiated in December 1964, Barrel Roll missions were flown against troops, equipment and supplies provided by North Vietnam in support of the Communist-led Pathet Lao.

Combat Beaver — An air concept developed by the Air Staff in conjunction with the other services during September-November 1966. It was designed to support a proposed electronic and ground barrier system between North and South Vietnam.

Flaming Dart — The initial Navy and Air Force retaliatory air strikes against North Vietnam on 7-8 and 11 February 1965.

Gate Guard — An air program designed to slow North Vietnamese infiltration toward the demilitarized zone. It began on 1 May 1966 in the northern part of Laos and then shifted into route package area I in North Vietnam.

Iron Hand — Operations begun in August 1965 to locate and destroy Soviet-provided SA-2 missile sites in North Vietnam.

Rolling Thunder — The major air campaign begun on 2 March 1965 which inaugurated regularly scheduled air strikes against North Vietnam.

Steel Tiger — Initiated in April 1965, Steel Tiger strikes were made against infiltration routes south of the 17th parallel in Laos.

Tally-Ho — An air interdiction program started on 20 June 1966 in the southern part of North Vietnam, aimed at slowing the infiltration of North Vietnamese troops, equipment, and supplies through the demilitarized zone into South Vietnam.

Tiger Hound — Begun in December 1965, these strikes were aimed at infiltration targets in southern Laos. They featured for the first time in Laos the use of forward air controllers and airborne command and control for certain strikes.

Wild Weasel — USAF aircraft, largely F-100F's and F-105F's, specially equipped with electronic and other devices to neutralize or destroy Soviet-provided SA-2 sites in North Vietnam.

CONTENTS

FOREWORD

NOTE

I. OBJECTIVES OF THE AIR WAR AGAINST NORTH VIETNAM 1

    Background to Rolling Thunder 1
    The Air Force and JCS Urge Early Renewed Bombing 4
    Secretary McNamara's Views 7
    The Bombing Resumes and Further Air Planning 9

II. INCREASING THE AIR PRESSURE ON NORTH VIETNAM 14

    Air Operations and Analyses 14
    The Beginning of Rolling Thunder Program 50 18
    The Rolling Thunder Study of 6 April 22
    Air Operations in May: Beginning of Gate Guard 25
    Highlights of June Operations 27

III. THE POL STRIKES AND NEW ROLLING THUNDER PROGRAM 51 . . . 29

    Background of the POL Air Strikes 29
    The Strikes of 29 June 31
    The Mid-1966 Assessment 33
    The Beginning of Rolling Thunder Program 51 35
    The Tally-Ho Air Campaign 38

IV. ANALYSES OF THE AIR CAMPAIGN 43

    Operational Studies 43
    The Effectiveness of Air Power 45
    Studies on Aircraft Attrition 49
    The Hise Report 52
    Secretary McNamara's Proposal to Reduce Aircraft Attrition . . . 56

V. THE AIR WAR AT YEAR'S END 58

    Approval of Rolling Thunder Program 52 59
    The Furor over Air Strikes "on Hanoi" 60
    Other Air Operations in November and December 62
    Assessment of Enemy Air Defenses 63
    Assessments of the Air War Against North Vietnam 67

NOTES 72

APPENDICES 82
    Appendix 1 - U.S. and VNAF Attack Sorties in Southeast Asia 82
    Appendix 2 - B-52 Sorties in Southeast Asia 82
    Appendix 3 - U.S. and VNAF Attack Sorties in North Vietnam 83
    Appendix 4 - U.S. Aircraft Losses in Southeast Asia 84
    Appendix 5 - USAF Combat Attrition in North Vietnam 85
    Appendix 6 - U.S. Aircraft Losses to SA-2's 85
    Appendix 7 - SA-2 Sites in North Vietnam 86
    Appendix 8 - Light and Medium Antiaircraft Artillery Guns
                 in North Vietnam. 86
    Appendix 9 - U.S. Aircraft Losses in Aerial Combat 87
    Appendix 10 - North Vietnamese Aircraft Losses in Aerial Combat 87

GLOSSARY 88

MAP 3
    Route Package Areas, North Vietnam 3

CHART 64
    Chronology of the Growth of North Vietnam's Air Defenses 64

I. OBJECTIVES OF THE AIR WAR AGAINST NORTH VIETNAM

From its inception, the "out-of-country" air campaign in Southeast Asia, that is, against targets in North Vietnam and Laos, was limited in scope and objective. The first air strikes against North Vietnam were conducted on 5 August 1964 by Navy aircraft in retaliation for Communist attacks on U.S. ships in the Gulf of Tonkin. The next ones occurred on 7-8 and 11 February 1965 when USAF and Navy aircraft flew "Flaming Dart" I and II missions in retaliation for Viet Cong assaults on U.S. military bases in South Vietnam. These were followed by an air program against selected North Vietnamese targets in order to exert, slowly and progressively, more military pressure on the Hanoi regime. Designated "Rolling Thunder," it began on 2 March 1965. As explained by Secretary of Defense Robert S. McNamara, the air attacks had three main purposes: raise South Vietnamese morale, reduce the infiltration of men and supplies to South Vietnam and increase its cost, and force the Communists at some point to the negotiating table.*

Background to Rolling Thunder

The Rolling Thunder program was basically a USAF-Navy air effort but included occasional token sorties by the Vietnamese Air Force (VNAF). Adm. U.S. Grant Sharp, Commander-in-Chief, Pacific (CINCPAC), Honolulu, exercised operational control through the commanders of the Pacific Air Forces (PACAF), the Seventh Fleet, and the Military Assistance, Command, Vietnam (MACV). Coordination control was assigned to the PACAF commander with the tacit understanding that it would be further delegated to Maj. Gen. Joseph H. Moore, Jr.,

---
* For highlights of the air war against North Vietnam and Laos prior to 1966, see Jacob Van Staaveren, <u>USAF Plans and Policies in South Vietnam and Laos,</u> (AFCHO, 1964), and <u>USAF Plans and Operations in Southeast Asia,</u> (AFCHO, 1965).

commander of the 2d Air Division (predecessor of the Seventh Air Force) in South Vietnam. Both the Air Staff and the PACAF commander considered this arrangement inefficient, believing that air assets in Southeast Asia, with few exceptions, should be under the control of a single Air Force commander.[1]

With the air program carefully circumscribed, the North Vietnamese initially enjoyed extensive sanctuaries. These included the Hanoi-Haiphong area and the northeastern and northwestern portions of the country closest to China. Targets were selected by the Joint Chiefs of Staff (JCS) after considering the recommendations of Admiral Sharp and the MACV commander, Gen. William C. Westmoreland, the decisions being based on intelligence from the war theater and in Washington. The Secretary of Defense reviewed the recommendations and then submitted them to the President for final approval. Special targeting committees performed this vital task.[2]

Rolling Thunder at first was characterized by individually approved air strikes but, as the campaign progressed, the high authorities approved one- and two-week target "packages" in advance and also gradually expanded the bombing area. In August 1965 they narrowed North Vietnam's sanctuaries to a 30-nautical mile radius of Hanoi, a 10-nautical mile radius of Haiphong, a 25-nautical mile "buffer" near the Chinese border extending from the coast to longitude 106° E. and a 30-nautical mile buffer from longitude 106° E. westward to the Laos border. By early September armed reconnaissance sorties had reached a rate of about 600 per week and did not rise above this figure during the remainder of the year. There was a reduction in the number of fixed targets that could be hit[*] and no extension of the bombing area. Poor weather contributed to the static sortie rate after September.[3]

---

[*] However, the list of 220 fixed targets as of 20 September was not reduced.

ROUTE PACKAGE AREAS
NORTH VIETNAM
22 Apr 66

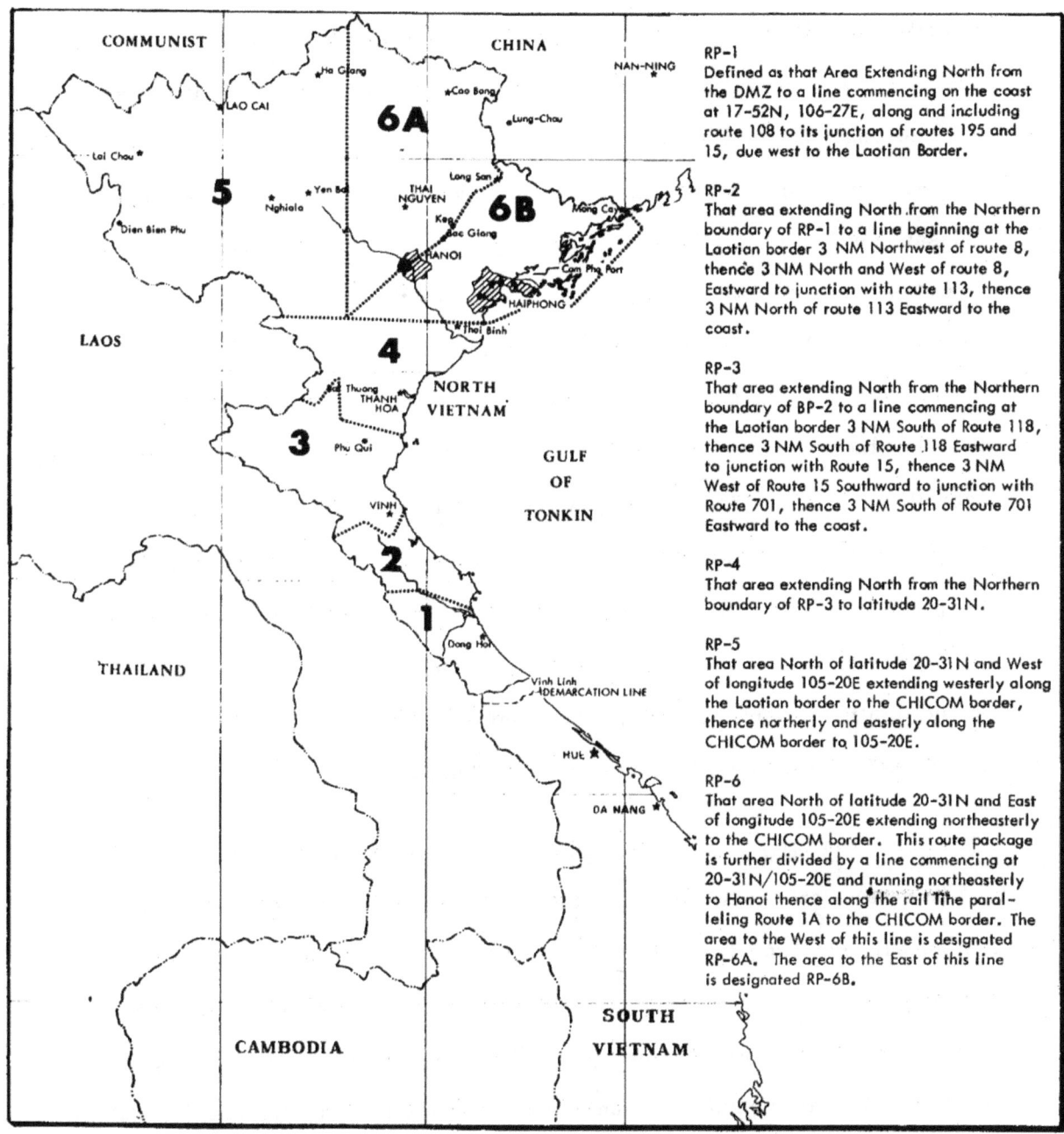

RP-1
Defined as that Area Extending North from the DMZ to a line commencing on the coast at 17-52N, 106-27E, along and including route 108 to its junction of routes 195 and 15, due west to the Laotian Border.

RP-2
That area extending North from the Northern boundary of RP-1 to a line beginning at the Laotian border 3 NM Northwest of route 8, thence 3 NM North and West of route 8, Eastward to junction with route 113, thence 3 NM North of route 113 Eastward to the coast.

RP-3
That area extending North from the Northern boundary of BP-2 to a line commencing at the Laotian border 3 NM South of Route 118, thence 3 NM South of Route 118 Eastward to junction with Route 15, thence 3 NM West of Route 15 Southward to junction with Route 701, thence 3 NM South of Route 701 Eastward to the coast.

RP-4
That area extending North from the Northern boundary of RP-3 to latitude 20-31N.

RP-5
That area North of latitude 20-31N and West of longitude 105-20E extending westerly along the Laotian border to the CHICOM border, thence northerly and easterly along the CHICOM border to 105-20E.

RP-6
That area North of latitude 20-31N and East of longitude 105-20E extending northeasterly to the CHICOM border. This route package is further divided by a line commencing at 20-31N/105-20E and running northeasterly to Hanoi thence along the rail line paralleling Route 1A to the CHICOM border. The area to the West of this line is designated RP-6A. The area to the East of this line is designated RP-6B.

Source: USAF Mgt Summary, 22 Apr 66

In November 1965 there was an important change in bombing procedure when Admiral Sharp, at the Navy's request, divided North Vietnam into six principal "route packages." Each included lines of communication (LOC's) and other targets suitable for armed reconnaissance strikes and were to be assigned to the Air Force or Navy for a two-week period, the duration of specific Rolling Thunder programs at that time. (Service air strikes against fixed JCS-numbered targets were excepted and took precedence over armed reconnaissance operations.) Starting 10 December, the Air Force began armed reconnaissance flights in route packages II, IV, and V, and the Navy in route packages I and III.* General Moore, commander of the 2d Air Division, was dissatisfied with this split system of air responsibility. He felt it continued to forfeit the advantages of centralized air control under which the complementing capabilities of Air Force and Navy aircraft could be better coordinated.[4]

(U) On 24 December 1965 the Americans began a two-day Christmas bombing pause in the air campaign against the North which eventually grew into a 37-day moratorium as the U.S. government made a major effort to find a basis for negotiating an end to the war. The limited bombing of targets in Laos and the air and ground war in South Vietnam continued, however.[5]

The Air Force and JCS Urge Early Renewed Bombing

Both the Air Staff and the USAF Chief of Staff, Gen. John P. McConnell, were deeply troubled by the bombing moratorium. Testifying before Senate committees early in January 1966, General McConnell observed that it enabled Hanoi to move men, supplies, and equipment around the clock and to restore its lines of communication. A delay in resuming attacks could

---
* With variations, the rotation policy continued until April 1966. See p 21.

prove costly in lives. Concerned about the relative ineffectiveness of the 1965 bombing effort, he favored removing political restraints on the use of air power to allow heavier strikes before a major U.S. and allied force buildup, then under consideration by the administration, was approved. He thought that the military effort against North Vietnam should have a priority equal to that given by the administration to the war in the South.[6]

(TS-GP 3) Other service chiefs supported General McConnell's recommendations to resume and intensify the bombing of the North. On 8 January 1966 they informed Secretary McNamara that the bombing pause was greatly weakening the U.S. negotiating "leverage" and proving advantageous to Hanoi, permitting it to reconstitute its forces and continue infiltration through Laos into South Vietnam. They recommended renewed bombing 48 hours after a Soviet delegation, then in Hanoi, returned to Moscow. Concerned about a possible Communist misinterpretation of U.S. resolve, the Joint Chiefs wanted to insure that any peace negotiations were pursued from a position of strength.[7]

(S-GP 3) After a Central Intelligence Agency (CIA) and Defense Intelligence Agency (DIA) analysis confirmed that the 1965 bombings had failed to halt the resupply of Communist forces, the JCS prepared another recommendation for Secretary McNamara. On 18 January it urged, again in accordance with General McConnell's view, that the bombing moratorium end with a "sharp blow" followed by expanded air operations throughout the North. It suggested reducing the "sanctuary" areas to a 10-nautical-mile radius of Hanoi and Phuc Yen airfield, a 4-nautical mile radius of Haiphong, and a 20-nautical-mile "buffer" zone in the northeast and northwest areas near the Chinese border. The JCS also called for closing the major seaports (by mining) and removing other political restraints against striking important targets.[8]

On 25 January, in answer to a query from Secretary McNamara, the JCS proposed three alternate ways to resume the bombing. One would use all Thai-based USAF aircraft and planes from three Navy carriers, flying 450 sorties per day for 72 hours, hitting all land and water targets (vehicles, ferries, pontoon bridges, etc.) outside of the sanctuary areas. The second would use the same aircraft flying armed reconnaissance against all LOC and petroleum, oil, and lubricants (POL) targets for 24 to 72 hours with follow-on attacks in accordance with the first alternative. The third called for 600 armed reconnaissance sorties per week in southern North Vietnam with the tempo being increased until the target program recommended on 18 January was reached.[9]

In addition to their proposals to renew the bombing, the Joint Chiefs examined ways to improve air activity. They sent Admiral Sharp guidance on making more effective air strikes against watercraft on inland waterways in the North. Until the bombing halt, more watercraft had been observed as air attacks on the road and rail network had forced the North Vietnamese to rely increasingly on water transportation. The Joint Chiefs concluded that better air-delivered mines should be developed and asked the Chief of Naval Operations (CNO) to give special attention to this matter.[10]

The JCS also examined the problem of closing down the 124-mile rail link between Hanoi and Lao Cai. This and the Hanoi Dong Dang line were the two principal rail arteries to the Chinese border. Secretary McNamara had expressed surprise that the Hanoi-Lao Cai segment was still in service despite repeated air strikes by USAF aircraft before the bombing pause. On 22 January, the JCS chairman, Gen. Earle G. Wheeler responded that there were two reasons why it remained open: frequent aborts because of weather during

December 1965 -- amounting to 37 percent of the planned sorties that month -- and the arrival of Chinese railway engineering personnel that substantially augmented the North Vietnamese repair capability. To keep the line closed, said General Wheeler, would require the destruction of three bridges, at least 100 armed reconnaissance sorties per week, and the use of reliable, long-delay bomb fuzes and seismic fuze antirailroad mines, both still under development.[11]

Secretary McNamara's Views

(U) The administration moved cautiously toward a decision on whether to renew the bombing of the North. On 19 January Secretary McNamara informed the Joint Chiefs that their views on this matter were under constant study by the State Department. On the 26th, in a summation of the 1965 Rolling Thunder program, the Defense Secretary told a House subcommittee:[12]

> It was clearly recognized that this pressure, by itself, would not ever be sufficient to cause North Vietnam to move toward negotiation unless it were accompanied by military action in South Vietnam that proved to the North that they could not win there. These were our objectives then; they are our objectives now. A corollary of these objectives is the avoidance of unnecessary military risk. We, therefore, have directed the bombing against the military targets, primarily routes of infiltration.
>
> We have not bombed Hanoi, we have not bombed Haiphong. We have not bombed certain petroleum supplies which are important. We have not mined the Haiphong port. We have gradually evolved from last February to mid-December, a target system that included all of North Vietnam except certain specified locations.
>
> The targets were very carefully chosen and the rate at which the bombing program grew was very carefully controlled, all for the purpose of trying to achieve our limited objective without widening the conflict.

(U) It was also Secretary McNamara's "strong personal opinion" that the war in South Vietnam could not be won solely by bombing the North and that the northern air campaign should be essentially a "supplement" to military action in the South.[13]

Although the air war was carefully limited, the Defense Secretary informed the President that it had already achieved the objective of raising the cost of infiltration. Air attacks had reduced the amount of enemy supplies reaching the South, carried mostly by trucks over greatly improved routes, from about 400 to 200 tons per day. Moreover, they had diverted 50,000 to 100,000 personnel* to air defense and repair work, hampered the mobility of the populace, forced decentralization of government activities thus creating more inefficiency and political risk, and reduced North Vietnam's activities in Laos.

For 1966, Secretary McNamara thought that the bombing "at a minimum" should include 4,000 attack sorties per month consisting of day and night armed reconnaissance against rail and road targets and POL storage sites except in cities and the buffer zone near the Chinese border. He proposed more intense bombing of targets in Laos, along the Bassac and Mekong rivers running into South Vietnam from Cambodia, and better surveillance of the sea approaches. In the South there should be more harassment of enemy LOC's and destruction of his bases.

Recognizing that estimates of enemy needs and capabilities and the results of air action "could be wrong by a factor of two either way," the Secretary advised the President that unless studies under way indicated otherwise, heavier bombing probably would not put a tight ceiling on the enemy's activities in South Vietnam. However, he thought it would reduce the flow of Communist supplies and limit the enemy's flexibility to undertake frequent offensive action or to defend himself adequately against U.S., allied,

---

* Estimates on the size of air defense and repair crews varied widely during 1966. See pp 34, 47, and 69.

and South Vietnamese troops. Mr. McNamara suggested two possible by-products of the bombing effort: it should help to condition Hanoi toward negotiation and an acceptable end to the war and it would maintain the morale of the South Vietnamese armed forces. The defense chief also outlined for the President the 1966 military objectives for South Vietnam.*[14]

The Bombing Resumes and Further Air Planning

(U) Having received no acceptable response from Hanoi to his peace overtures, President Johnson on 31 January ordered resumption of the bombing of North Vietnam. It began the same day. "Our air strikes... from the beginning," the President announced, "have been aimed at military targets and controlled with great care. Those who direct and supply the aggression have no claim to immunity from military reply." Other officials told newsmen that the United States would continue to limit bombing of the North but intensify other aspects of the war, including more use of B-52 bombers and ground artillery in South Vietnam.[15]

As anticipated, the bombing moratorium had in fact benefited the North Vietnamese. USAF reconnaissance revealed that supplies had moved by truck and rail 24 hours per day and that repairs and new construction on the road and rail net likewise had proceeded on a "round-the-clock" basis. General McConnell believed that the moratorium had permitted the North to

---

* The objectives were formalized during a meeting between President Johnson, and South Vietnamese Prime Minister, Nguyen Cao Ky at Honolulu from 6 to 8 February. They agreed to try to: (1) raise the casualty rate of Viet Cong-North Vietnamese forces to a level equal to their capability to put new men in the field; (2) increase the areas denied to the Communists from 10 to 20 percent to 40 to 50 percent; (3) increase the population in secure areas from 50 to 60 percent; (4) pacify four high-priority areas containing the following population: Da Nang, 387,000; Qui Nhon, 650,000; Hoa Hao, 800,000, and Saigon, 3,500,000; (5) increase from 30 to 50 percent the roads and rail lines open for use; and (6) insure the defense of all military bases, political and population centers, and food-producing areas under the control of the Saigon government.

strengthen its antiaircraft defenses, including expansion of its SA-2 system from about 50 to 60 sites. Admiral Sharp reported the enemy had deployed about 40 more air defense positions in the northwest rail line area and 26 more guns to protect routes south of Vinh.[16]

When the aerial attacks resumed as Rolling Thunder program 48, allied air strength in South Vietnam and Thailand consisted of about 689 U.S. and 125 Vietnamese Air Force tactical combat aircraft.* More would arrive in subsequent months. The limitations placed on the renewed bombing effort disappointed the Joint Chiefs, especially since none of their recommendations had been accepted. In fact, the program was more restrictive than before the bombing pause. Armed reconnaissance during February was limited to 300 sorties per day and almost solely to the four route package areas south of Hanoi. Only one JCS target, Dien Bien Phu airfield, was hit several times. Poor weather forced the cancellation of many strikes and others were diverted to targets in Laos. A Pacific Command (PACOM) assessment indicated that the renewed air effort was producing few important results as compared to those attained during 1965 against trucks, railroad rolling stock, and watercraft.[17]

Meanwhile, the bombing policy remained under intensive review. At the request of Secretary McNamara, General Wheeler on 1 February asked the service chiefs to establish a joint study group which would examine again the Rolling Thunder program and produce data that could serve as a basis for future JCS recommendations. They quickly organized the group under the leadership of Brig. Gen. Jammie M. Philpott, Director of Intelligence,

---

* The number of U.S. tactical combat aircraft by service were: Air Force, 355; Navy (three carriers), 209; and Marine Corps, 125. In addition the Air Force had 30 B-52's in Guam. (North Vietnam possessed about 75 MIG's.)

Strategic Air Command (SAC). Its report was not issued until April.*[18]

On 8 February, following a three-week conference of service officials in Honolulu to plan U.S. and allied air and ground deployments, through fiscal year 1968, Admiral Sharp and his staff briefed Secretary McNamara on the results of their deliberations. They proposed a program of stepped up air attacks in the North and in Laos with the immediate goal of destroying Communist resources contributing to the aggression, and of harassing, disrupting, and impeding the movement of men and materiel. Admiral Sharp advocated 7,100 combat sorties per month for the North and 3,000 per month for the South.[19]

Secretary McNamara did not immediately respond to these sortie proposals. However, he approved, with certain modifications, CINCPAC's recommended schedule for additional air and ground forces. These deployments promised to strain severely the resources of the services, especially those of the Air Force and the Army. Concerned about their impact on the Air Force's "roles and missions," force structure, overall posture, and research and development needs, Lt. Gen. H.T. Wheless, Assistant Vice Chief of Staff on 18 February directed Headquarters USAF's Operations Analysis Office to undertake a "vigorous" analysis and asked all Air Staff offices to support the effort. Its major purpose was to develop a more comprehensive data base on the use of air power in Southeast Asia.[20]

Because of the decision to deploy more forces and the likelihood of stepped up air and ground operations, General McConnell decided a number of organizational changes were necessary. He directed the Air Staff to replace the 2nd Air Division with a numbered Air Force, upgrade the

---
* See p 22.

commander of the Thirteenth Air Force in the Philippines to three-star rank, and formalize USAF-Army airlift arrangements in the theater.*²¹

With the air campaign continuing at a low tempo, the JCS, with Air Staff support, reaffirmed its prior recommendation to Secretary McNamara for accelerated air operations against the North and to strike all targets still under administration wraps. If this could not be approved, the JCS urged extending operations at least to the previously authorized areas. The Joint Chiefs warned that if more remunerative targets could not be hit to compensate for the handicaps imposed by operational restraints, more air sorties should be flown elsewhere. They also raised their estimated sortie requirement for the northern campaign from 7,100 to 7,400 per month, citing Admiral Sharp's newly acquired intelligence which confirmed additional enemy deployments of SA-2 missiles and possible Chinese antiaircraft artillery units in the northeast region.²²

Secretary McNamara informed the JCS that the political atmosphere was not favorable for implementing these recommendations. Some Air Staff members attributed the administration's cautiousness to the Senate Foreign Relations Committee hearings on the war, which began 4 February under the chairmanship of Senator J. William Fulbright. In addition, the Defense Secretary was known to believe that there were limitations to what air power could do in the type of war being waged in Southeast Asia. Mr. McNamara thought that even the obliteration of North Vietnam would not completely end that country's support of enemy operations in the South since most of the arms and ammunition came from other Communist nations. He firmly believed

---

* See Van Staaveren, 1966, p 40.

that the war would have to be won on the ground in South Vietnam.[23]

(U) Secretary of the Air Force Harold Brown echoed this administration position position, asserting publicly on 25 February that the destruction of the North's remaining industrial capacity would neither prevent the resupply of equipment and troops in the South nor end hostilities. He also said:[24]

> . . . should it appear that we were trying to destroy North Vietnam, the prospect of escalation by the other side would increase, and with it would increase the possibility of heavier U.S. casualties and an even harder and longer war . . . .
>
> . . . our objective is not to destroy North Vietnam. It is to stop aggression against South Vietnam at the lowest feasible cost in lives and property. We should take the course that is most likely to bring a satisfactory outcome . . . at a comparately low risk and low cost to ourselves. Our course is to apply increasing pressure in South Vietnam both by ground and supporting air attacks; to make it clear to the North Vietnamese and Viet Cong forces . . . that life is going to get more difficult for them . . . that war is expensive and dangerous.

(U) Thus, for the time being, the JCS-recommended program for an accelerated air campaign against North Vietnam had no chance of receiving administration approval.

II. INCREASING THE AIR PRESSURE ON NORTH VIETNAM

On 1 March the JCS generally endorsed Admiral Sharp's "Case I"* air, ground, and naval deployment program leading to stepped-up operations against the Communists in North and South Vietnam and Laos. It also recommended again that the war be fought in accordance with the Concept for Vietnam paper which it had approved on 27 August 1965 and later amended. This paper called for air strikes against the North's war-supporting industries in the Hanoi-Haiphong area, aerial mining of the ports, additional interdiction of inland and coastal waterways, and special air and ground operations in Laos -- all recommended many times in various ways. But administration authorities continued to favor a more modest air effort against the Hanoi regime.¹

Air Operations and Analyses

The new Rolling Thunder program -- number 49 -- was ushered in on 1 March. It was still limited to armed reconnaissance of the North but the administration had broadened the authorized attack area to include coastal regions and had eased restrictions to permit the use of air power up to the level existing when bombing ceased on 24 December 1965. The Air Force and Navy were allocated a total of 5,100 armed reconnaissance sorties (and 3,000 for Laos), with the number to be flown by each contingent on weather and other operational factors. Poor weather, however, limited their sorties to 4,491 during the month. The Air Force concentrated its efforts against targets in route packages I, III, and VIA, the Navy in route

---

* Case I called for deployment of a total of 413,557 U.S. personnel in South Vietnam by the end of calendar year 1966.

packages II and IV and against coastal targets in route package I through IV. The VNAF flew token sorties in route package I under the protection of U.S. Marine Corps electronic and escort aircraft. On 10 March the JCS again pressed for its proposed accelerated air program with early attacks on POL sites, the main rail system running from China, and the mining of deep water ports. Again the recommendation was not acted upon.[2]

Meanwhile, the North's air defense system began to pose a greater threat to USAF and Navy operations. On 3 March photo reconnaissance aircraft discovered about 25 MIG-21 fuselage crates at Phuc Yen airfield near Hanoi. USAF "Big Eye" EC-121D aircraft also detected airborne MIG's about 55 times during March, although there were no engagements. Admiral Sharp directed the PACAF and Seventh Fleet commanders to prepare for counter-air operations and the SAC commander to submit a plan for a B-52 strike, if necessary, against Phuc Yen and Kep airfields.* He asked for additional electronically equipped USAF EB-66 aircraft to reduce the effectiveness of the SA-2 missiles and the anti-aircraft guns. "Jamming" was thought to have already reduced the usefulness of enemy air defenses.[3]

Aircraft losses to enemy ground fire continued to cause much concern. A Joint Staff study of the problem during March showed that 199 American aircraft had been lost over North Vietnam since the bombings began on 7 February 1965, sixteen of them by SA-2 missiles.

---

* Gen Curtis E. LeMay, former CSAF, first recommended striking the North's airfields on 10 August 1964 and the JCS sent its first recommendation to do so on 14 November 1964. By 1 March 1966 the JCS had made a total of 11 such recommendations but the administration had approved strikes on only three small airfields at Vinh, Dong Hoi, and Dien Bien Phu in May 1965, June 1965, and February 1966 respectively.

The aircraft loss rate was six times higher in the northeast, the most heavily defended area, than in the rest of North Vietnam. Headquarters USAF estimated the North's antiaircraft strength at 2,525 guns.*[4]

To improve its analysis of aircraft losses and other operational data, the Air Staff on 26 March established an <u>ad hoc</u> study group in the Directorate of Operations. In the same month the Chief of Operations Analysis, in response to General Wheless' directive of 17 February, completed an initial study on the effectiveness of air interdiction in Southeast Asia. It summarized the enemy's supply requirements, his capability to transport supplies by land or sea, and the extent air strikes had hampered such activities. One conclusion was that air attacks had not yet decreased the movement of men and supplies from the North through Laos to South Vietnam. They had, however, inflicted about $15 to $16 million direct and $8 million indirect damage on the North's economy and forced Hanoi to recruit 30,000 more personnel, in addition to local forces, to perform repair work. An analysis of one route from Vinh to Muang Phine suggested that air attacks had caused the Communists to increase their truck inventory by one-third and their transport time by two-thirds.[5]

Another Operations Analysis interdiction study listed enemy targets destroyed or damaged in North Vietnam and Laos through March 1966 as follows:

---

* Estimates of North Vietnam's antiaircraft gun inventory varied considerably during 1966. See Admiral Sharp's estimate of July, p 34, the Seventh Air Force's estimate for January and December 1966, p 64, and a final estimate, app 8.

	North Vietnam			Laos		
	Des	Dam	Total	Des	Dam	Total
Transportation Vehicles	1,537	2,500	4,307	515	485	1,000
LOC Network *	546	4,381	4,927	398	4,886	5,284
Counter-Air +	134	189	323	145	67	145
All Other ++	3,681	4,196	7,877	2,783	1,259	3,997
Total	5,898	11,266	17,164	3,841	6,697	10,426

Concerning the Communist effort to fill craters and repair roads damaged by air attacks, there were indications that only one man-day of direct productive effort per attack sortie was needed to perform this task. "At this rate," the Operations Analysis study observed, "a few hundred sorties per day would only make enough work for a few hundred men."

As for Communist supplies, the study estimated that in 1965 they averaged 51 tons per day across the North Vietnamese-Laos border and 16 tons per day across the Laos-South Vietnamese border. For 1966 (through March), the figures were 70 and 35 tons respectively. The Laos panhandle infiltration routes in themselves appeared to be capable, despite air attacks, of supporting the current low-level combat by Viet Cong and North Vietnamese forces. To support a higher combat level, for example, one day in seven, the Communists would have to use other supply channels or dip into South Vietnamese stockpiles, either of which would complicate their distribution problems.[6]

* Included bridges, road cuts, rail cuts, ferry ships.

+ Included aircraft, runways, antiaircraft sites, SA-2 sites, and radar sites.

++ Included buildings, POL tanks, power plants, locks and dams.

The Beginning of Rolling Thunder Program 50

Concurrently, there was planning for the next Rolling Thunder program. In meetings with General Wheeler on 21 and 23 March, Secretary McNamara set forth certain guidelines for stepping up air strikes in the northeast and hitting additional JCS targets. The Joint Chiefs quickly responded by proposing Rolling Thunder program 50. It called for launching 900 attack sorties against major lines of communication and striking nine POL storage areas, six bridges, one iron and steel plant, one early warning and ground control intercept (EW/GCI) site, and one cement plant, the latter in Haiphong. Admiral Sharp planned to conduct this program within an allocation of 8,100 sorties (5,100 for North Vietnam, 3,000 for Laos).[7]

Administration authorities approved this program, which began on 1 April. For the first time in 1966 armed reconnaissance was authorized over the far northeast and four new JCS targets (all rail and highway bridges) were cleared for interdiction. However, some time before program 50 ended on 9 July, permission to strike the other JCS-recommended targets was withdrawn. Dissatisfied with the restrictions, General McConnell and the Marine Corps chief jointly advised the JCS that "sound military judgment" dictated that all the targets be hit immediately. Higher administration officials withheld consent, however, principally because of the unstable South Vietnamese political situation which developed after the ruling junta's ouster on 10 March of Lt. Gen. Nguyen Chanh Thi, the I Corps commander.[8]

Poor weather in April again limited the number of attack sorties flown against the North and delayed until 5 May the completion of strikes against the four authorized JCS targets. Other air operations included armed reconnaissance against roads, rail lines, watercraft and similar LOC targets. April also saw several important developments: establishment of the Seventh Air Force, the first B-52 strike in North Vietnam, a marked step-up in Hanoi's air defense effort that resulted in a U.S. downing of the first MIG-21, a change in the command and control of route package I, and the beginning of a study on increasing air pressure to offset civil disturbances in South Vietnam.[9]

The establishment of the Seventh Air Force, effective 8 April, followed General McConnell's successful efforts to raise the stature of the major USAF operational command in the theater. General Moore continued to serve as its chief with no change in his relationship with other commanders. Also, in accordance with General McConnell's wishes, the commander of the Thirteenth Air Force in the Philippines was raised to three-star rank on 1 July.[10]

SAC made the first B-52 strike against the North on 12 April when 30 bombers dropped 7,000 tons of 750- and 1,000-pound bombs on a road segment of Mugia Pass near the Laotian border. It was believed to be the single greatest air attack on a target since World War II. Initial reports indicated that "route 15" had been "definitely closed" by a landslide as had been hoped; however, 26 1/2 hours later reconnaissance photos showed all the craters filled in and the road appeared serviceable, attesting to the quick repair capability of the North Vietnamese. A second strike by 15 B-52's on 26 April on a road segment six kilometers north of Mugia blocked the road for only 18 hours. The apparent inability of the B-52's to close down the road -- expressed by the Secretary of State and other officials -- and a Seventh Air Force report of an SA-2 site near Mugia, prompted Admiral Sharp on 30 April to recommend to the JCS no further attacks on the pass.

In fact, the bombers were not again used near North Vietnam until 30 July.*[11]

Towards the end of April Hanoi stepped up its air defense activity, dispatching 29 to 31 MIG's against USAF and Navy aircraft. In nine separate engagements in five days, six MIG's were destroyed, all by USAF F-4C's which suffered no losses. The first MIG-21 was downed on 26 April by two F-4C's. Antiaircraft fire continued to account for most American aircraft combat losses with 31 downed (14 USAF, 17 Navy), while two -- an F-102 and a Navy A-1H -- were struck by SA-2 missiles.[12]

Meanwhile, a change in command and control of air operations in route package I followed a meeting on 28 March between Admiral Sharp and the JCS. The PACOM commander recommended that General Westmoreland's request for partial operational control of this area be approved and that the sector be accorded the same priority as for South Vietnam and Laotian "Tiger Hound" air operations. General Westmoreland urgently desired more air power to hit enemy approaches to the battlefield area near the Demilitarized Zone (DMZ) for which he was responsible. Admiral Sharp thought that 3,500 sorties a month was warranted alone for route package I.[13]

USAF commanders and the Air Staff objected to the proposed change, feeling that MACV's command authority should be limited to South Vietnam. They believed that the PACAF commander should remain the sole coordinating authority for the Rolling Thunder program. Nevertheless, Secretary McNamara approved the change on 14 April and the JCS endorsed it on the 20th. To allay any doubts where he thought the war's emphasis should be, the defense chief said that air operations north of route package I could be carried out only if they did not penalize air operations in the

---

* See p 40.

"extended battlefield," that is, in South Vietnam, the Tiger Hound area of Laos, and route package area I. Under this change Admiral Sharp still retained partial operational control of route package I. General Westmoreland's authority was limited to armed photo reconnaissance and intelligence analysis of Rolling Thunder and "Iron Hand" operations. Simultaneously, the Air Force-Navy rotational bombing procedure in other route packages, in effect since late 1966, also ended.*[14]

The civil disturbances and reduced U.S. and allied military activity in both South and North Vietnam that followed General Thi's dismissal+ prompted the Joint Staff on 14 April to recommend a step-up in the attacks in accordance with the JCS proposals of 18 January. It thought this might help arrest the deteriorating situation. A special Joint Staff study of the problem also examined the possibility that a government coming to power in Saigon might wish to end the war and ask U.S. and allied forces to leave.[15]

The Air Staff generally supported the Joint Staff's recommendation for an intensified air offensive against the North and withdrawal of U.S. forces if a local _fait accompli_ left the United States and its allies no choice. But the Army's Chief of Staff doubted that heavier air strikes could resolve the political situation in South Vietnam. Observing that Admiral Sharp already possessed authority to execute some of the recommended strikes, he opposed sending the Joint Staff's study to Secretary McNamara on the grounds that if U.S. strategy was to be reevaluated it should be by separate action. General McConnell suggested, and the JCS agreed, to consider alternate ways of withdrawing part or all of the U.S.

---

* See p 4.

+ See p 18.

forces from South Vietnam should this be necessary. Reviews were begun but in subsequent weeks, after political stability was gradually restored, the need to consider withdrawal action lessened and no final decisions were taken.[16]

The Rolling Thunder Study of 6 April

(U) April also witnessed the completion of the special joint report on the Rolling Thunder program requested by Secretary McNamara in February. Prepared under the direction of General Philpott,[*] it was based on all data available in Washington plus information collected by staff members who visited PACOM, MACV, the 2d Air Division, and the Seventh Fleet.

Completed on 6 April, the Philpott report reviewed the results of one year of Rolling Thunder operations (2 March 1965-2 March 1966). During this period U.S. and VNAF aircraft had flown about 45,000 combat and 20,000 combat support sorties, damaging or destroying 6,100 "fixed" targets (bridges, ferry facilities, military barracks, supply depots, etc.), and 3,400 "mobile" targets (trucks, railroad rolling stock, and watercraft). American combat losses totaled about 185 aircraft.

The report touched briefly on Laos where the air effort consisted primarily of armed reconnaissance in two principal areas designated as "Barrel Roll" and "Steel Tiger." It noted that the effectiveness of USAF strikes in Laos was limited because of small fixed targets, high jungle growth, and mountainous terrain that hampered target location and identification. Also, important targets were normally transitory and had to be confirmed carefully before they could be attacked. The operations in North Vietnam and Laos, said the report:

---
* See pp 10-11.

> . . . have achieved a degree of success within the parameters of imposed restrictions. However, the restricted scope of operations, the restraints and piecemealing effort, have degraded program effectiveness to a level well below the optimum. Because of this, the enemy has received war-supporting materiel from external sources, through routes of ingress, which for the most part have been immune from attack, and has dispersed and stored this materiel in politically assured sanctuaries. . . . Although air operations caused significant disruption prior to the standdown, there has been an increase in the North Vietnamese logistic infiltration program, indicating a much greater requirement for supplies in South Vietnam. . . .

Of a total of 236 "JCS numbered" targets in North Vietnam, 134 had been struck, including 42 bridges. Among the 102 untouched targets, 90 were in the northeast area and, of these, 70 were in the sanctuary zones of Hanoi, Haiphong, and the "buffer" territory near China. Elsewhere in the North 86 percent of the JCS targets had been hit. The report further asserted:

> The less than optimum air campaign, and the uninterrupted receipt of supplies from Russia, China, satellite countries, and certain elements of the free world have undoubtedly contributed to Hanoi's belief in ultimate victory. Therefore . . . the Study Group considers it essential that the air campaign be redirected against specific target systems, critical to the capability and important to the will of North Vietnam to continue aggression and support insurgency.

It consequently proposed a three-phase strategy. In Phase I, over a period of four to six weeks, the United States would expand the armed reconnaissance effort over the North except for the sanctuary areas and again attack previously struck JCS-numbered targets in the northeast. Air units also would strike 11 more JCS-numbered bridges, and the Thai Nguyen railroad yards and shops; perform armed reconnaissance over Kep airfield; strike 30 more JCS-numbered targets, 14 headquarters/barracks, four ammunition and two supply depots, five POL storage areas, one airfield, two naval bases, and one radar site.

In Phase II, a period of somewhat less duration than Phase I, American aircraft would attack 12 military and war-supporting targets within the reduced sanctuary areas, consisting of two bridges, three POL storage areas, two railroad shops and yards, three supply and storage depots, one machine tool plant, and one airfield. During Phase III all remaining JCS-numbered targets (now totaling 43) would be attacked, including six bridges, seven ports and naval bases, six industrial plants, seven locks, 10 thermal/hydroelectric plants, the headquarters of the North Vietnamese ministries of national and air defense, and specified railroad, supply, radio, and transformer stations.

Concurrent with this program, the study group proposed three attack options that could be executed at any time: Option A, strike the Haiphong POL center; Option B, mine the channel approaches to Haiphong, Hon Gai, and Cam Pha; and Option C, strike four jet airfields -- at Phuc Yen, Hanoi, and Haiphong.

Finally, it proposed that Admiral Sharp should determine when to hit the targets in each of the three phases, the weight of the air attacks, and the tactics to be employed.[17]

General Wheeler, who was briefed on the report on 9 April, called it a "fine professional approach," a "good job," and endorsed it. The manner in which it should be sent to Secretary McNamara created difficulties, however. General McConnell suggested that the Joint Staff prepare "positive" recommendations for the implementation of the report's air program, stating that if this were not done, it would not receive the attention it deserved. But strong service support was lacking for that approach. An agreement eventually was reached to send the report to

Secretary McNamara with the Joint Chiefs "noting" it. They advised him it was fully responsive to his request, was in consonance with the JCS recommendations of 18 January 1966, and would be useful in considering future recommendations of the Rolling Thunder program.[18]

Air Operations in May: Beginning of "Gate Guard"

(U) The Rolling Thunder study had no immediate impact on air operations. In fact, Secretary Brown on 22 May publicly affirmed the administration's decision not to expand significantly attacks on new targets. He said such action would not cut off infiltration but would raise the danger of a wider war.*[19]

Thus the authorized level of 5,100 sorties for North Vietnam remained unchanged in May and only a few important attacks on fixed targets were approved. The principal operation was against seven targets within the Yen Bai logistic center which were struck by 70 USAF sorties. Monsoon weather again plagued the air campaign, causing the cancellation of 2,972 USAF-Navy sorties or about 32 percent of those scheduled. USAF sortie cancellations amounted to 40 percent.[20]

Heavier North Vietnamese infiltration toward the DMZ as indicated by more truck sightings led to a change in tactics. Beginning on 1 May, a special air effort called "Gate Guard" was initiated in the northern part of the Steel Tiger area in Laos and then shifted into route package I when the monsoons hit the Laotian region. Utilizing many of the "integrated interdiction" tactics developed in Laos earlier in the year, Gate Guard involved stepped-up air strikes on a series of routes or "belts"

---

* Not stated by Secretary Brown was the fact that civil disturbances in South Vietnam triggered by the dismissal of General Thi on 10 March still prompted the administration not to risk escalation of the war at this time. See p 18.

running east to west. Many special USAF aircraft were used: C-130 airborne command and control centers, C-130 flare aircraft, EB-66's for ECM, and RF-101's. Attack aircraft interdicted selected points in daytime and destroyed "fleeting targets" at night.[21]

During the month there were few MIG sightings and only one was destroyed. Heavy antiaircraft fire accounted for most of the 20 U.S. aircraft (13 USAF, six Navy, one Marine) that were downed. USAF losses included seven F-105's in the northeast. The enemy's ground fire, General McConnell informed a Senate subcommittee during the month, was "the only thing we are not able to cope with . . ." whereas the SA-2's -- which were deployed at about 103 sites -- had destroyed only five USAF and two Navy aircraft. The SA-2's were countered by decoys, jamming techniques, and evasive aircraft tactics.*[22]

During May the Air Staff began a study effort to establish requirements for a suitable, night, all-weather aircraft interdiction system using the latest munitions, sensors, and guidance equipment to provide an "aerial blockade" against infiltrating men and supplies. This followed an expression of frustration by high State Department and White House officials in late April about the inability of air power to halt these movements into the South. As part of this study, the Air Staff solicited the views of PACAF, SAC, and other commands, advising them of the need for a solution within existing bombing restraints. Recommendations to "strike the source" of Communist supplies, they were informed, were politically unacceptable and likely to remain so.[23]

---
* Air Force confidence in the value of anti-SA-2 operations was challenged in a Seventh Fleet study, dated 12 July 1966 and based on SA-2 USAF and Navy firing reports. It asserted that the value of ECM and other jamming techniques was uncertain as aircraft with deception devices normally sought to evade the missiles when fired upon. For General Harris' view, see pp 53-54.

In a joint reply on 24 May, the commanders-in-chief of PACAF and SAC, Generals Hunter Harris, Jr. and John D. Ryan, pointed to improved results from air operations in route package I and in parts of Laos. They said that interdiction could become even more effective by greater use of air-delivered mines (against ferries), "denial" munitions with delayed fuzes insuring "longevity" up to 30 days, around-the-clock air strikes on selected routes south of Vinh, special strikes against Mugia Pass, and improved air-ground activity in Laos. They also proposed the use of low-volatile chemical-biological agents to contaminate terrain and surface bursts of nuclear weapons. The latter would "dramatically" create "barriers" in areas difficult to bypass. To implement these measures, General Harris again stressed the need for centralized control of air resources, asserting it should be a "high priority" Air Force objective. But most of these suggestions could not or would not be implemented in the immediate future.[24]

Highlights of June Operations

June witnessed another step-up in air activity over North Vietnam, the major highlight being USAF-Navy strikes, beginning 21 June, against previously exempt POL storage sites and culminating in major POL strikes in Hanoi and Haiphong on the 29th. (See details in Chapter III.)

3) Other targets continued to be hit, such as the Hanoi-Lao Cai and Hanoi-Dong Dang rail lines, but most USAF sorties concentrated on route package I targets which absorbed about 93 percent of the total flown in the North that month. These strikes reflected the importance General Westmoreland placed on curbing the flow of enemy troops and supplies toward and into the DMZ. Gate Guard targets were hit hard and, after the introduction of USAF MSQ-77 "Skyspot" radars for greater bombing

accuracy,* the infiltration "gates" were "guarded" virtually around the clock. About 97 percent of the Navy effort was concentrated along the coast in route packages II, III, and IV. The VNAF flew 266 sorties in route package I, its highest total against the North in 12 months.[25]

The Gate Guard campaign seemed to confirm the value of night air attacks. By 7 July the nightime missions had achieved better results than those in daytime, 164 trucks being destroyed and 265 damaged compared with the daytime toll of 154 destroyed and 126 damaged.[26]

Despite these successes, Gate Guard operations faced certain handicaps. During daylight hours USAF O-1 forward air control (FAC) aircraft -- used to support U.S. strikes -- were highly vulnerable to the heavy ground fire and, when forced to fly higher, became less effective. Also, interdiction points, often on flat terrain, were easy to repair or by-pass. And the North Vietnamese could store and service their trucks in numerous small villages, secure in the knowledge that U.S. aircraft would not attack civilian areas. Events finally overtook the Gate Guard effort. Continued infiltration through the DMZ prompted Headquarters MACV to develop a "Tally-Ho" air program -- a more ambitious effort to block, if possible, a large-scale invasion by North Vietnamese troops through the DMZ into South Vietnam's northernmost provinces.[27]

---

* The initial MSQ-77 radar was placed at Bien Hoa, South Vietnam on 1 April 1966, and the second one at Pleiku in May. With the installation of the third and fourth radars at Nakhon Phanom, Thailand and Dong Ha, South Vietnam on 3 and 12 June, respectively, the system could be used for air strikes in route package I. A fifth radar was placed at Dalat, South Vietnam on 26 September. The MSQ-77 was an MSQ-35 bomb-scoring radar converted into a bomb-directing radar with a range of 200 nautical miles.

III. THE POL STRIKES AND ROLLING THUNDER PROGRAM 51

As indicated, the highlight of the air war -- and of the Rolling Thunder program since its inception -- were the POL strikes in June 1966. General McConnell and the other service chiefs had long urged the destruction of North Vietnam's major POL sites but the administration did not seriously consider attacking them until March.

Background of the POL Air Strikes

Some months before, in December 1965, a CIA study had concluded that the destruction of the North's POL facilities would substantially increase Hanoi's logistic problems by requiring alternate import and distributing channels and the use of more rail cars, drums, and other storage items. CIA analysts recognized that the North Vietnamese probably anticipated such attacks and that the POL facilities near Haiphong, a major port city, politically were sensitive targets. Assessing the consequences of a POL air campaign, they further concluded it would (1) not change Hanoi's policy either toward negotiation or toward sharply entering the war; (2) probably result in more Soviet pressure on the regime to negotiate; (3) force Hanoi to ask for and receive more supply and transport aid from China and air defense aid from the Soviet Union; (4) aggravate Soviet-Chinese relations, and (5) cause further deterioration of U.S.-Soviet relations, especially if a Soviet ship were hit. Soviet counteraction was thought possible and might take the form of attacks on U.S. ferrett aircraft or interference with U.S. access to West Berlin. Chinese Communist intervention in the war, while possible, was considered unlikely.[1]

In March another CIA study predicted that the destruction of POL sites (and a cement plant in Haiphong) would severely strain the North's transportation system. It was one of the most influential documents to bear on the subject. On 23 March Secretary McNamara informed General Wheeler that a new Rolling Thunder program directed against POL storage and distribution targets might be favorably received. On 25 April, Deputy Secretary of Defense Cyrus R. Vance assured the JCS that its 1965 POL studies were now receiving full consideration. On 6 May, a White House aide, Walt W. Rostow, recalling the impact of oil strikes on Germany in World War II, suggested to the Secretaries of State and Defense that systematic and sustained bombing of POL targets might have more prompt and decisive results on Hanoi's transportation system than conventional intelligence indicated.* 2

On 31 May -- although a final decision to hit the major facilities had not been made -- Admiral Sharp was authorized to attack certain POL-associated targets in the northeast along with five small route targets. On 6 June General Westmoreland advised CINCPAC that an improving political situation in South Vietnam (since civil disturbances began on 10 March) was causing Hanoi much disappointment and dismay. Noting this circumstance and the heavy toll inflicted by the air campaign over North Vietnam and Laos, he recommended that these psychological and military gains be "parlayed into dividends" by hitting the POL storage sites. To do so later, he warned, would be less effective because of dispersal work already under way.³

Support continued to build up. Admiral Sharp quickly endorsed General Westmoreland's views and, on 8 June, the U.S. Ambassador

---
* Mr. Rostow observed that in 1965 U.S. estimates showed that 60 percent of the North's POL was for military purposes and 40 percent for civilian needs. The current ratio was now placed at 80 and 20 percent, respectively.

to South Vietnam, Henry Cabot Lodge suggested that intensified bombing was the most effective way to get Hanoi to the negotiating table. General McConnell, who had long supported such action, told a Senate subcommittee that hitting POL targets would have a "substantial" effect on the amount of supplies the Communists could send to their forces in South Vietnam. An Air Staff intelligence report asserted that hitting the sites would have "a most profound" impact on Hanoi's infiltration activities and expressed confidence it could be done without causing severe civilian casualties.[4]

The Strikes of 29 June

The administration now moved toward its decision. In a preliminary action, the JCS on 16 June authorized Admiral Sharp to hit all of the POL dispersal sites listed in the current Rolling Thunder program except those within a 30-nautical-mile radius of Hanoi, a 10-nautical-mile radius of Haiphong, and 25 nautical miles from the Chinese border east of longitude $105° 20'$ E. and 30 nautical miles west of longitude $105° 20'$ E. On 21 June USAF jets struck gasoline and oil depot sites ranging from 28 to 40 miles from Hanoi. Several other sites, previously exempt from attack, were hit in ensuing days outside the Hanoi-Haiphong area.[5]

In addition, extraordinary steps were taken to prepare for the attacks on POL targets in the two main cities of North Vietnam. On 23 June, after Secretary McNamara and General Wheeler had informed President Johnson of their precautionary measures* to avoid attacks on civilian areas

---

* Nine "rules" were laid down: use of pilots most experienced with operations in the target areas, weather conditions permitting visual target identification, avoiding to the extent possible populated areas, minimum pilot distraction to improve delivery accuracy, use of munitions assuring highest precision consistent with mission objectives, attacks on air defenses only in sparsely populated areas, special security precautions concerning the proposed operations, and personnal attention by commanders to the operations.

and foreign merchant ships, the JCS authorized Admiral Sharp to strike early on the 24th seven POL storage facilities and a radar site at Kep, northeast of Hanoi. Although special security precautions surrounded the planning, the news media soon reported the essential details of the operation. This forced the administration to postpone it and deny any decision had been made.[6]

The strike was rescheduled and took place on 29 June. A USAF force of 24 F-105's, 8 F-105 "Iron Hand's", 4 EB-66's plus 24 F-4C's and 2 F-104's for MIG "cap" and escort hit a 32-tank farm about three-and-a-half miles from Hanoi. Approximately 95 percent of the target area, comprising about 20 percent of the North's oil storage facilities, was damaged or destroyed. Simultaneously, Navy A-4 and A-6 aircraft hit a large POL storage area two miles northwest of Haiphong. This facility, containing an estimated 40 percent of the North's fuel storage capacity and 95 percent of its unloading equipment, was about 80 percent destroyed. One USAF F-105 was lost to ground fire. Four MIG-17's challenged the raiders and one was probably shot down by an Iron Hand F-105. No SA-2 missiles were observed. Maj. Gen. Gilbert L. Myers, deputy commander of the Seventh Air Force termed the raids "the most significant, the most important strike of the war." Secretary McNamara subsequently called the USAF-Navy strike "a superb professional job," although he was highly incensed over the security leaks that preceded the attacks.[7]

(U) In a press conference the next day, the defense chief said the strikes were made "to counter a mounting reliance by North Vietnam on the use of trucks and powered junks to facilitate the infiltration of men and equipment from North Vietnam to South Vietnam." He explained that truck movements in the first five months of 1966 had doubled, and that daily supply tonnage and troop infiltration over the "Ho Chi Minh trail" were up 150 percent and 120 percent, respectively, over 1965. Further, the enemy had built new roads and its truck inventory by December 1966 was expected to be double that of January 1965. This would require a 50- to 70-percent increase in oil imports over 1965. The Secretary also justified the timing of the strikes, asserting that the "perishable" nature of POL targets made it more desirable to attack them now than earlier in the year.[8]

President Johnson said that the air strikes on military targets in North Vietnam "will continue to impose a growing burden and a high price on those who wage war against the freedom of others." He directed that in the forthcoming weeks first priority be given to "strangling" the remainder of Hanoi's POL system except for that portion in areas still exempt from air attack. He also wanted more bombing of the two main rail lines running between Hanoi and China.[9]

The Mid-1966 Assessment

Shortly after the 29 June POL strikes, another major conference took place in Honolulu to review the war and plan additional U.S. and allied air, ground, and naval deployments. A mid-year assessment of the war, contained in a letter from Admiral Sharp to the JCS and the Office of the Secretary of Defense (OSD), was expanded in briefings for Mr. McNamara in Honolulu on 8 July. The PACOM commander said that he considered the air program for North Vietnam still inadequate, observing that previous recommendations to hit major ports of entry, logistic targets leading from China, and certain POL sites (in addition to those struck on 29 June) had not been approved. He thought it impossible to prevent the enemy from moving supplies from North to South and thus to "isolate the battlefield"; rather, the "highest task" was route interdiction and striking new targets as they were uncovered. Recent intelligence showed that the air campaign was hurting Hanoi. Its repair and reconstruction force now totaled about 500,000 and the morale of the government and troops was declining. To raise the cost of infiltration, he proposed striking as soon as possible 33 important exempted targets and more of the enemy's supplies, road and rail repair centers, and military training areas.[10]

Admiral Sharp pointed to Hanoi's greater effort to hide and disperse its logistic supplies because of the air attacks. As a result there was greater U.S. effort in the first six months of the year to uncover more of the following types of targets:

	1 Jan 66	1 Jul 66	Total New Targets
Truck Parks	55	126	121
Military Storage Facilities	316	696	380
POL	38	180	142
Military Installations	680	939	259
Transshipment Points	7	65	65
Total	1,096	2,006	967

The table showed an increase of 90 percent in significant targets since 1 January 1966 with the major portion consisting of truck parks, military storage facilities, and transshipment points.

During the first half of the year, Admiral Sharp continued, Rolling Thunder strikes had destroyed or damaged 1,076 trucks, 900 pieces of rolling stock, and 3,304 watercraft. A total of 2,771 trucks were destroyed or damaged in Laos. Discussing the North's air defense system, he said that Hanoi's antiaircraft gun inventory had increased from about 859 in February 1965 (when the bombings began) to more than 4,200,[*] an average increase of about 205 guns per month. The North also possessed 20 to 25

---

[*] See pp 16 and 63-65, and app 8.

active SA-2 battalions, good early warning, ground control interception equipment, and a respectable MIG force.[11]

In reply, Secretary McNamara reported that President Johnson had accorded first priority to "strangulation" of the North's POL system. Thus, it was essential to determine Hanoi's land and sea distribution system, categorize the targets, and then render them ineffective. The Secretary also pointed out the need for increased interdiction of railroad lines, particularly bridges in the northeast and northwest leading to China. Expressing concern over U.S. aircraft attrition, he said OSD was working with the services on ways to reduce it.[12]

The Beginning of Rolling Thunder Program 51

The strangulation campaign was incorporated into a new Rolling Thunder program -- number 51. It was authorized by the JCS on 6 July and went into effect on the 9th. Armed reconnaissance could now encompass all of North Vietnam except for the established sanctuary areas (i.e., a 30-nautical-mile radius of Hanoi, a 10-nautical-mile radius of Haiphong, and 25 to 30-nautical-mile buffer area adjacent to China). Admiral Sharp assigned PACAF specific responsibility for halting all rail traffic in the northeast and northwest sectors. In addition, the JCS on 9 July authorized an increase in attack sorties for North Vietnam and Laos from 8,100 to 10,100 per month.[13]

Because of the high priority assigned to the strangulation effort -- and in response also to Secretary McNamara's direction -- the Air Staff on 16 July established an Operation Combat Strangler task force headed by Maj. Gen. Woodrow P. Swancutt, Director of Operations, Headquarters USAF. Its immediate objective was to evaluate POL strangulation and LOC interdiction plans prepared by the Seventh Air Force and PACAF. Simultaneously, the Air Staff established an Operations Review Group within the Directorate of Operations under Col. LeRoy J. Manor, an enlarged and reorganized successor to the ad hoc study group formed on 26 March 1965.* It examined the effectiveness of combat and combat support operations in Southeast Asia as well as the activities of USAF worldwide operational forces.[14]

Under Rolling Thunder program 51, USAF aircraft intially concentrated on route packages I, V, and VIA and the Navy on the others. Then on 20 July, at the direction of General Westmoreland, the Air Force inaugurated a "Tally-Ho" air campaign in route package I in a renewed effort, somewhat similar to Gate Guard, to curb Communist infiltration into and through the DMZ. Also, on 6 August at General Westmoreland's request and by the decision of Admiral Sharp, the "Dixie Station" aircraft carrier used for air operations in South Vietnam was moved to "Yankee Station," thereby providing three rather than two carriers for the stepped up air activities against the North. Another important change was an agreement between the Seventh Air Force and Seventh Fleet commanders whereby the former would provide about 1,500 sorties per month in the normally Navy-dominated route packages II, III, and IV. The Air Staff and General Harris considered the arrangement better than the relatively rigid delineation of service air responsibility for the North that had existed previously. Although the agreement took effect on 4 September+, restrictions on air operations east of "route 15" prevented its full realization.++ [15]

---

* See p 16.

\+ By September USAF aircraft generally were covering 46,265 square miles or 77 percent of the land area of North Vietnam. The Navy, by comparison, was covering 13,891 square miles or about 23 percent of the land area.

++ The restrictions were eased in December 1966.

The immediate priority, of course, was given to POL sites. The campaign increased in momentum until the week of 13-19 August when 140 attack sorties were flown against POL targets. Thereafter the sortie rate dropped. By the end of August an estimated 68 percent of known POL storage capacity in route packages I, V, and VI had been destroyed. On 19 September the remaining POL capacity in the North was placed at about 69,650 metric tons, of which 18,526 metric tons were not yet authorized for destruction.[16]

By the end of September it was apparent that the POL strikes were becoming less productive. There had been no let-up in Soviet deliveries of POL supplies and the North Vietnamese continued their dispersal efforts. Supported by Combat Strangler analyses, PACAF considered the benefits derived from attacking the scattered sites no longer worth the cost in aircraft lost. In a report to Secretary Brown on 14 October, PACAF stated that the POL campaign had reached the point of diminishing returns and that the Soviet Union and China could adequately supply the North with POL products. Also, U.S. air power could best force changes in POL handling and distribution by striking targets listed in Rolling Thunder program 52 proposed by the JCS on 22 August.* This would constitute, PACAF felt, the best kind of "strategic persuasion" before Hanoi could devise countermeasures.[17]

The railroad strangulation effort, particularly against the Hanoi-Lao Cai and the Hanoi-Dong Dang lines running to China and located in route packages V and VI A, was not especially productive because of bad weather and the ability of the North Vietnamese to repair the lines quickly. In fact,

---

* This program called for 872 sorties over 19 new targets.

PACAF believed it was virtually impossible to maintain an effective air program against them. Weather problems in the two route packages forced the cancellation or diversion of about 70 and 81 percent of the attack sorties scheduled for July and August, respectively. The weather improved in September but turned poor again in October.[18]

Enemy antiaircraft defense, including additional SA-2's also added to the difficulty in interdicting the two main rail lines. As American aircraft losses rose, Admiral Sharp on 20 September ordered a reduction of about one-third of the air strikes in route package VIA until measures could be devised to reduce the toll. For example, on 7 August antiaircraft guns knocked down seven U.S. aircraft (six USAF, one Navy), the highest one-day total since 13 August 1965 when six were shot down. American combat losses in the North during the third quarter of the year were: 41 in July, 37 in August, and 26 in September. Eighty of these were USAF aircraft. In October combat losses declined to 23, only nine of them USAF.[19]

MIG pilots also became increasingly aggressive. Fifteen "incidents" in July resulted in two MIG-21's and one MIG-17 being shot down against the loss of one USAF F-105 and one Navy F-8. During an engagement on 7 July, two MIG-21's for the first time in the war fired air-to-air missiles against two F-105's but failed to score. Another milestone in the air war occurred on 21 September when the biggest air-to-air battle to date was fought over the North. In seven separate encounters USAF pilots downed two MIG-17's, probably a third, and damaged a MIG-21 without suffering any losses.[20]

<u>The Tally-Ho Campaign</u>

In terms of total sorties flown, the largest portion of the USAF effort, as in previous months, was concentrated in route package I which included the DMZ, the area of the greatest enemy threat. Intelligence believed that about 5,000 North Vietnamese had infiltrated through the zone in June. PACAF speculated that these enemy movements may have been due to the recent success of Tiger Hound air operations in Laos which, together with monsoon weather, had virtually blocked certain logistic routes in that country.[21]

As more enemy troops pressed toward the DMZ and intelligence reported that the North's 324 "B" Division of 8,000 to 10,000 men, had crossed over into the I Corps area of South Vietnam, General Westmoreland asked Lt. Gen. William W. Momyer, who succeeded General Moore as Seventh Air Force commander on 1 July, to prepare an air program similar to Tiger Hound in Laos for the most southern part of route package I including the zone. Already under way just south of the DMZ was a combined U.S. Marine and South Vietnamese Army and Marine air and ground effort called Operation Hastings. General Momyer quickly outlined a "Tally-Ho" air campaign against enemy targets in an area about 30 miles inside North Vietnam from the Dai Giang river below Dong Hoi through the DMZ to its southern border. The first Tally-Ho air strike was made on 20 July by USAF and Marine aircraft, the latter beginning regular operations in the North for the first time.* Like Gate Guard, C-130 airborne control was employed and, for the first time, USAF O-1 FAC's flew into North Vietnam to help find targets. To sustain Tally-Ho, Tiger Hound activity in Laos was scaled down.[22]

Although Tally-Ho included the DMZ, military operations

---

* Previously Marine Corps activities in the North consisted of eight sorties in April and two sorties in June.

within the zone were not conducted immediately. The political problems associated with such action had been under study for some time. On 20 July, the day Tally-Ho began, the JCS finally authorized Admiral Sharp to launch air or artillery strikes in the southern half of the zone. This followed protracted State and Defense Department negotiations which resulted in State's approval if the allies had concrete evidence that the North was using the zone for infiltrating men and materiel, if there existed an adequate record of the Saigon government's protest to the International Control Commission (ICC)[*] concerning Hanoi's violation of the zone, and if an appropriate public affairs program was begun prior to military action in the zone.[23]

After these conditions were fulfilled, the JCS on 28 July specifically authorized B-52 strikes in the southern portion of the DMZ in support of U.S.-South Vietnamese "self-defense" operations. In their first attack there, on 30 July, 15 B-52's dropped bombs on ammunition dumps, gun positions, and weapon staging targets. In August B-52's returned there several times.[24]

On 22 August General McConnell informed Secretaries Vance and McNamara of a rising trend in USAF out-of-country night operations, especially in North Vietnam, and of his expectation that the trend would continue in the Tally-Ho campaign. But shortly thereafter the hazards of antiaircraft fire and inadequate aircraft control forced a reduction in the use of USAF O-1 FAC's and, consequently, of other combat aircraft. In fact, the night attack effort, despite General McConnell's hopes, did not show a significant rise again until December.[25]

---

[*] The ICC, composed of representatives from India, Canada, and Poland, was established in July 1954 as a result of the Geneva conference that ended the French-Indochina war. Its primary function was to supervise the 1954 Geneva agreements.

In September the advent of better weather and better results with the use of MSQ-77 radar permitted intensification of the Tally-Ho operations. Many secondary explosions often followed USAF-Marine Corps air strikes. The first B-52 strike in the northern portion of the DMZ was made on 16 September and others soon followed until 26 September when they were halted in the zone east of route package I to permit ICC inspection of North Vietnamese troop infiltration. As the Communists continued to use this area, administration authorities on 13 October rescinded the prohibition against air and artillery strikes. On the 14th B-52 strikes were stopped in the zone, this time because of the danger from suspected SA-2 sites.[26]

Tally-Ho continued through October and into November. As in the Gate Guard operations, Tally-Ho FAC pilots often were forced up to 1,500 feet by ground fire, thus reducing the value of visual reconnaissance. They also experienced severe turbulence over mountainous terrain and poor weather added to their difficulties.[27]

The Tally-Ho program remained under constant review. Initial evidence appeared to show that its operations destroyed many enemy structures, supplies, antiaircraft positions, and vehicles, and that it hampered but did not stop infiltration on foot through the DMZ. On 10 October, during a briefing for Secretary McNamara and other top officials who were visiting Saigon, Brig. Gen. Carlos M. Talbott of the Seventh Air Force indicated that Tally-Ho and other air activities possibly had caused the enemy to reach the limit of his supply capability. PACAF officials thought that Tally-Ho and U.S.-South Vietnamese "spoiling" attacks in and below the DMZ had thwarted a major offensive planned by the North Vietnamese into the I Corps. On the 13th, the JCS, in answer to a White House request for an assessment of the enemy threat in the zone, likewise reported that spoiling attacks and tactical and

B-52 air strikes in and near the demilitarized area had defeated the North Vietnamese and prevented them from seizing the initiative. But the service chiefs warned that the enemy still retained considerable offensive capability and that U.S. reinforcements should be sent to that region.[28]

However, these were general observations. The USAF Vice Chief of Staff, Gen. Bruce K. Holloway, when pressed by Secretary Brown on the effect of the air effort on North Vietnamese movement through the DMZ, was less certain about the results of Tally-Ho operations. He replied: "I do not know what the effect is and nobody else seems to know," adding that there was much "speculation and excuses why it's hard to determine." He said that there were several actions under way to improve data-gathering in the DMZ area. These included establishing a tactical air support analysis team (TASAT) composed of 20 Air Force and Army personnel to insure systematic data-reporting, forming a similar USAF-Army team to assess B-52 strikes, inviting the Army and Navy to join the Air Force Combat Strangler task force in assessing the results of the air campaign, and organizing an air weapon survey board.[29]

The need for more reliable information on Tally-Ho activities near the DMZ was also reflected in the observation of a USAF intelligence officer in South Vietnam who was associated with the air campaign. "We don't know how effective we were," he commented, "for we don't know what we stopped or the amount of flow." He thought the program could be made more productive by defoliating the terrain and by improving intelligence, targeting, and communication procedures. Subsequently, a list of targets believed to have been damaged or destroyed by the Tally-Ho program was compiled.*[30]

---

* See p 62.

IV. ANALYSES OF THE AIR CAMPAIGN

The beginning of Rolling Thunder program 51 also witnessed the start of a greater Air Staff effort to analyze the effectiveness of USAF operations in Southeast Asia, particularly in North Vietnam. With the assignment of more personnel in July to the Operations Review Group under Colonel Manor and Operation Combat Strangler under General Swancutt, the Air Force improved its ability to collect and evaluate operational data and to respond to requests from higher authorities for information on different aspects of the air war.

Operational Studies

One of the early important products of the Swancutt task force was its analysis of the Seventh Air Force POL and LOC air campaign against North Vietnam. Completed on 30 August, it pointed to the inflexibility of air operations in the North. This situation was attributed to seven main factors: air restrictions that reduced aircraft maneuver, the prohibition against striking certain target areas, the "route package" system that divided into relatively independent regions the USAF and Navy target areas of responsibility, a targeting system that had the effect of concentrating air power and thus "telegraphing" U.S. intentions to the enemy, bad weather and anti-aircraft defenses that left little choice in tactics, the existence of few profitable targets, and fragmented command and control of air activities.

Based upon its analysis, the task force recommended two primary changes: a broadened target base to allow an increase in the tempo of air operations and a single centralized command and control system for air. It also began assembling a complete statistical record of aircraft losses, ordnance expended, results of air strikes, and tactics employed (because of the inordinately high aircraft losses in route packages V and VIA), and analyzing Seventh Air Force and PACAF plans weekly. The group also proposed that the Air Force seek permission for its aircraft to hit targets in the Navy-dominated route packages II, III, and IV when weather forced diversionary strikes, and it recommended more night air operations. Agreements subsequently were reached to allow USAF units to make diversionary air strikes in the Navy areas, the new policy becoming effective on 4 September.[1]

Also in August the Air Staff examined the value of air attacks on North Vietnamese watercraft. This was in response to a query from Secretary Brown who observed that Admiral Sharp, in his briefing of 8 July in Honolulu, had indicated that 2,358 watercraft had been attacked by air to that time.[2] General Holloway advised on 22 August that in Admiral Sharp's view, air strikes on largely coastal watercraft through mid-1966 had not always been worth the effort, although they did have a harassing effect on the North Vietnamese. Since July, because of the stepped up air operations on land transportation routes, a larger volume of barge traffic had appeared on inland waterways. In the Thanh Hoa and Vinh areas, watercraft construction was exceeding civilian needs. Some watercraft carried POL drums, tanks, and ammunition, and there were more attempts to camouflage them. Thus, said General Holloway, Admiral Sharp now believed that they were worthwhile air targets.[3]

On 13 September, again at the request of Secretary Brown, the Air Staff undertook a detailed study of the types of target systems in North Vietnam. The approach included an examination of the cost and the length of time needed to destroy a part or all of each target, and the effect its loss would have on Hanoi's ability to continue hostilities. The primary target systems being studied were electric power, maritime ports, airfields, navigation locks and dams, industrial facilities, command and control sites, extractive industries, military installations, and LOC's. The project had not been completed by the end of the year.[4]

The Effectiveness of Air Power

The Air Staff also assembled data to reply to numerous questions raised by Secretary McNamara on the effectiveness of air power. On 2 September, during a meeting with Air Force, Navy, and other officials, the defense chief asked the Air Force to examine the combat use of F-4C and F-105 aircraft. He wished to determine whether F-4C's should fly most of the sorties against North Vietnam, especially against "fleeting" night targets, and whether F-105's should be employed in South rather than North Vietnam. He also asked for a comparative study of the performance of propeller and jet aircraft in night operations over route packages I and II. From the Navy, Secretary McNamara wanted recommendations on how to increase the number of night sorties over North Vietnam.[5]

On the basis of data collected by the Air Staff, Secretary Brown advised the defense chief on 28 September that while the F-4C and F-105 aircraft were both suited for daytime attack missions, the F-4C was more effective at night, principally because it carried two pilots. This permitted better target-finding, better radar-controlled formations (by the rear pilot), and more protection for pilots against "spatial disorientation/vertigo." Although a switch in the use of the F-105 from North to South Vietnam would reduce its losses, other reasons militated against such a change. It would affect the logistical base of the two aircraft, probably not reduce aircraft attrition in route package areas V and VI (where enemy defenses were heaviest), and create an aircrew replacement problem. He supported the assigned missions of the two aircraft and the practice of "attriting" the F-105's first in order to conserve the F-4C's.

Secretary Brown reported that comparisons between propeller and jet aircraft in night operations were inconclusive because of vast differences in their use. In North Vietnam the Air Force used its A-1's in less defended areas while the Navy did not employ its A-1's until an area was first tested by A-4's. In Laos Air Force A-1 losses were higher because of lower attack speed or more ordnance-delaying passes against targets.[6]

The study requested by Secretary McNamara on stepping up night operations over North Vietnam was submitted by Navy Secretary Paul M. Nitze. He said more night sorties would cause a drop of about 15 percent in Navy attack efforts, reduce effectiveness by about 50 percent compared with daytime strikes, result in more civilian casualties, and double operational aircraft losses -- although combat losses would remain about the same. In view of these findings, and because he believed it was necessary to maintain pressure on the North "around the clock," Secretary Nitze recommended no change in the current "mix" of day and night sorties.[7]

Secretary McNamara also expressed dissatisfaction with the level of air analysis performed by the services, pointing to the differences between the estimates made in several studies on the effects that the POL strikes would have on North Vietnamese infiltration and those that actually occurred. He asked the Navy Secretary especially to review past CIA, DIA, and other reports on this matter as well as analyze the general subject of aircraft losses. He enjoined the Air Force to make more "sophisticated" analyses of the conflict, asserting that this was one of the "most important" things that it could do.[8]

On 3 November Secretary Nitze sent Mr. McNamara an initial report on the Navy's most recent air studies. The findings -- and admissions -- were unusual. He said the report showed that (1) there was insufficient intelligence data to produce a viable assessment of past or projected air campaigns; (2) North Vietnam's logistic requirements for forces in the South, compared with its capabilities, were small, thus permitting Hanoi to adjust the level of conflict to its available supplies; and (3) North Vietnam's estimated economic loss of $125 million versus $350 million of Soviet and Chinese aid taken alone, was a "poor trade-off" when compared with the cost of achieving the end product. The first two factors, the Navy Secretary observed, emphasized the magnitude of the task of disrupting North Vietnamese infiltration.

3) Admittedly, he continued, air attacks had produced some results such as requiring North Vietnam to provide for an air defense system and to maintain a 300,000-man road and bridge repair force that reduced resources available for infiltration into South Vietnam. And prisoner of war and defector reports testified to some success of the air and ground campaign in the South. Nevertheless, because of the inadequacy of available data, analysts were unable to develop a logical case for or against the current air campaign at either a higher or lower level. "This is not a criticism of the analytical effort," said Mr. Nitze, "rather, it is a reflection of the degree to which decisions in this area must be dependent on judgments in the absence of hard intelligence."

The Nitze report included a review of studies -- including the March 1966 CIA study which preceded and led to the U.S. decision to attack North Vietnam's POL system. The overall purpose of the air strikes had been to strain Hanoi's transportation system. Interviews with CIA analysts disclosed that many of their assumptions were based on certain estimates of the logistic capacity of the Hanoi-Dong Dang rail line, the amount of seaborne imports, the impact of hitting a cement plant in Haiphong, and other data. In retrospect, other factors also bore -- or could bear -- on the effectiveness of air operations against the enemy's logistic capability and resources, such as the existence of a road system parallel to the Hanoi-Dong Dang rail line, the construction by the Chinese of a new internal transport link to Lao Cai, the transport capacity of the Red River from Lao Cai to Hanoi, and the capability of the North Vietnamese to continue, although less efficiently, to produce cement in small, dispersed furnaces if the plant in Haiphong were destroyed.* There were indications that the analysts' use of 1965 average import statistics to project future North Vietnamese requirements resulted in an overstatement of Hanoi's needs. These -- and other examples -- showed the inadequacy of the information base for evaluating the effectiveness of air strike programs planned for North Vietnam.

To obtain better analyses for predicting the results of air strikes, the Nitze report indicated that the Chief of Naval Operations was establishing a special branch in the Navy's System Analysis Division to perform this vital task.[9]

---

* As the Haiphong plant was the only such facility in the North, the Air Staff seriously questioned the ability of the North Vietnamese to produce cement if it was destroyed.

Secretary Brown, in a reply to Mr. McNamara on 10 November, summarized current efforts to improve USAF analysis of the effectiveness of air interdiction. He cited the establishment in July of the Operation Combat Strangler task force and expansion of its functions to include development of a computer model to simulate air campaigns against North Vietnamese targets. The Air Force also was analyzing daily the air operations over North Vietnam, reviewing and evaluating major target systems including the anticipated effect of air attacks on the North's economy and on infiltration into the South, and studying the length of time required to destroy a given percentage of target systems and the cost of striking them in terms of sorties, munitions, and aircraft. This effort had been assigned top priority and the necessary resources. In addition to briefing the Air Staff, the task force made the various analyses available to the Joint Staff and OSD and posted pertinent data in a special situation room.

The Secretary of the Air Force also advised that the USAF study of major target systems in North Vietnam was 50 percent complete and would be finished early in 1967, after which a second analysis would "interface" all target systems to determine the cumulative effect of the destruction of several complimentary target systems. In addition, a special analysis of night operations was under way.[10]

Studies on Aircraft Attrition

Another problem area that received increased attention after mid-1966 was aircraft attrition. Following a USAF briefing on this subject on 6 June, Secretary McNamara asked the Air Force for a detailed analysis of losses.[11]

On 19 July Secretary Brown submitted coordinated USAF-Navy reply. Over North Vietnam, he said, the majority of aircraft losses (74 percent) were due to automatic weapon and light antiaircraft guns and most aircraft (77.1 percent) were hit below 4,000 feet. The losses were distributed fairly evenly over the route packages, with no meaningful differences in the loss rates by routes. He said an apparent USAF aircraft loss rate amounting to "three times" that of the Navy's was due principally to the lack of a clear definition of strike sorties, the limitations of the joint reporting system, and frequent diversion of sorties. Overall Air Force and Navy aircraft losses were quite similar, amounting to 3.96 and 4.32 aircraft per 1,000 sorties, respectively. He reported there was no data on the frequency of aircraft exposure to antiaircraft weapons at different altitudes, the proportion of losses sustained on each segment of an attack area, and the extent of increasing aircraft exposure to ground fire induced by avoiding SA-2 missiles.

An analysis of operational data for the period 1 October 1965 through 31 May 1966 by cause of loss, including "take-off" for combat missions, the Air Force Secretary continued, showed that by far most of the operational losses were due to aircraft system failures. The ratio of system failures to total operational losses in this period were by service: Air Force, 23 of 44; Navy, 10 of 29; and Marine Corps, three of nine. Of the 36 system failures, 22 involved aircraft engines, five were due to flight control problems, and the remainder were random system failures which occurred only once or twice. In addition, the Navy lost nine aircraft in carrier landings.

Compared with normal peacetime attrition, Secretary Brown added, actual operational losses in Southeast Asia for fiscal year 1966 were below predicted figures for USAF F-100's, F-104's, F-4C's and F-5's. Only F-105 losses were higher than expected and several efforts were under way, including a study by the Air Force Systems Command, to modify the aircraft in order to reduce combat losses. In addition to air crews, hydraulic-pneumatic systems (such as fuel and flight control) and aircraft engines were most vulnerable to enemy fire.[12]

At the request of Deputy Secretary Vance, the Air Force also made a special study of aircraft losses during night missions over North Vietnam and Laos. Reports submitted by Secretary Brown and General McConnell on 24 and 25 August showed that for the period 1 January - 31 July 1966, the aircraft loss rate per 1,000 sorties for night armed reconnaissance sorties averaged 0.84 compared to 4.27 for day armed reconnaissance. Night sorties were considerably less hazardous, primarily because North Vietnam's air defense weapons were largely optically directed.[13]

Aircraft losses remained of particular concern to the Air Staff since they threatened the Air Force's planned buildup to 86 tactical fighter squadrons by June 1968. On 29 August General Holloway, the Vice Chief of Staff, sent a report to General Wheeler on the effect of the losses on the Air Force's capabilities. It showed that at current aircraft loss rates the Air Force would be short five tactical fighter squadrons at the mid-point of fiscal year 1968 and three squadrons short at the end of the fiscal year. The approved squadron goal might not be reached until after the third quarter of fiscal year 1969. The report also indicated that an OSD-prepared aircraft "attrition model" needed adjustment to reflect more clearly sorties programmed for North Vietnam. It was on the basis of this model that OSD on 19 November 1965 had approved additional production of 141 F-4's to offset attrition. General Holloway said that the Air Staff would continue its analysis of this problem.[14]

(U) Aircraft attrition was, of course, being followed closely by administration officials and congressional critics. In recognition of the problem

Secretary McNamara on 22 September announced plans to procure in fiscal year 1968, 280 additional largely combat-type aircraft costing $700 million. Although the largest number were earmarked for the Navy, the Air Force would receive a substantial portion of the total.[15]

The Hise Report

Meanwhile, on 26 September, a Joint Staff study group completed a more detailed examination of aircraft attrition. Its findings were contained in the "Hise Report", named after the group's director, Marine Col. Henry W. Hise, whom General Wheeler had designated on 28 July to perform this task.*

The Hise group studied all factors affecting aircraft losses using data from joint operational reports, the DIA, and interviews with Air Force, Navy, and Marine commanders and airmen at Headquarters PACOM and in Southeast Asia. It covered all aircraft losses, whatever the cause, from January 1962 through August 1966. Totalling 814, the aircraft were lost in the following areas: North Vietnam, 363; Laos, 74; and South Vietnam, 377. The report analyzed the main factors affecting aircraft losses: time, enemy defenses, tactics, targeting, weather, sortie requirements, ordnance, aircrews, and stereotyped air operations.

The report's major conclusion was that North Vietnam had been given an opportunity to build up a formidable air defense system and noted, in support, General Momyer's recent observation: "In the past three months the enemy has moved to a new plateau of /air defense/ capability. He now has a fully integrated air defense system controlled from a central

---

* Some of the ground work of the Hise Report had been done by a study group headed by USAF Brig Gen. R.G. Owen at the request of General Wheeler on 25 April. The Hise study group consisted of four representatives -- one from each of the services, including USAF Col. C. L. Daniel -- and one representative from the DIA.

point in Hanoi." Both the antiaircraft guns and SA-2 missiles, according to the Hise Report, had had a "crippling effect" on air operations. The vast majority of aircraft losses were attributed to ground fire, with 85 percent of all "hits" being scored when the aircraft were below 4,500 feet. If Hanoi were permitted to continue its buildup of air defense weapons, the United States eventually would face a choice of supporting an adequate air campaign to destroy them, accepting high aircraft losses, or terminating air operations over the North.

The report also pointed to a number of other problems. It said that between 1 July and 15 September 1966 USAF's 354th TFS had experienced an inordinately high aircraft loss rate. Additionally, some pilots in the theater were overworked, several squadrons had fewer than authorized pilots, F-105 pilots had "low survivability" in route packages V and VIA, stereotyped operations contributed to air losses, and a larger stock of ordnance was needed to provide for a more intense antiflak program.[16]

General Harris on 20 October forwarded the PACAF-Seventh Air Force assessment of the Hise Report to General McConnell. He generally agreed with the report's conclusions about the buildup of the North's antiaircraft defenses and the need to broaden the target base. But he thought the report added little to a fundamental discussion of aircraft losses since it cited largely a number of well known facts. General Harris modified or took exception to a number of points raised. Concerning the effect of SA-2 missiles (which forced pilots down to within range of antiaircraft guns), he said that Air Force "Wild Weasel" and "Iron Hand" forces* equipped with electronic

---

* Wild Weasel aircraft, largely F-100F's and F-105F's, were specially equipped for anti-SA-2 operations. Iron Hand was the operational code name for attacks on SA-2 sites.

countermeasures (ECM) equipment were mitigating the effect of the SA-2's on tactics*, although a major development effort was still needed in this area. In bad weather it was the lack of an all-weather bombing system that limited operations rather than SA-2's. The Soviet-made missiles merely complicated bombings, making it difficult for aircraft to fly higher lest they become vulnerable to a missile hit.[17]

With respect to high losses incurred by the 354th TFS, General Harris attributed this primarily to aggressive leadership, accidents, and misfortunes in only one squadron -- something that often happened in peace as well as in war without identifiable causes. Nor did he consider overwork or fatigue of pilots a factor in aircraft losses. F-105 pilots at Takhli and Korat Air Bases in Thailand, for example, in July flew an average of 56.7 and 43.9 hours respectively. In August they flew 48.2 and 36.5 hours respectively. Although aircraft often flew twice in one day, pilots seldom did except during "peak loads" and this was an infrequent requirement.

General Harris also took issue with a statistical interpretation showing that F-105 pilots flying 100 missions over route packages V and VIA would suffer excessive losses. Although the figures (based on July and August data) were approximately correct, they represented the greatest attrition rate in a period of maximum losses in the highest risk area in Southeast Asia. Seventh Air Force records showed that only 25 percent of pilot missions were in high risk areas. Thus, in a 100-mission tour, an F-105 pilot would not lose his aircraft over enemy or friendly territory as often as alleged. He further observed that the F-4C loss rate was about one-fourth that of the F-105 rate. He conceded that some squadrons at Takhli and

---

* For General McConnell's and the Seventh Fleet's view of the effectiveness of anti-SA-2 operations. See p 26.

Korat Air Bases had been below authorized pilot strength during the June-September period.

The PACAF commander also agreed that, to some extent, there was a tendency to use standard or "stereotyped" tactics because of the need for efficient air scheduling and to meet JCS objectives. But it was North Vietnam's effective early warning and ground control interception system rather than stereotyped tactics that aided the enemy and provided him with nearly total information on U.S. air operations. The advantages of existing air scheduling, he thought, far exceeded the disadvantages.[18]

The Air Staff and General McConnell considered the data in the Hise Report as accurate and generally accepted the findings. On 10 October the JCS informed Secretary McNamara that, to the extent possible, Admiral Sharp and the services had taken several steps to ameliorate the aircraft loss rate. But certain other measures would require administration approval, particularly increased production of specific types of munitions for more effective suppression of enemy air defenses. There included 2.75 rockets with M-151 heads, Shrikes, CBU-24's, and 2,000- and 3,000-pound bombs. The Joint Chiefs reaffirmed their recommendation of 22 August that Rolling Thunder program 52 be adopted to broaden the target base over North Vietnam and make possible increased destruction of enemy air defense sites.[19]

The Hise Report findings prompted Dr. Brown and Deputy Secretary of Defense Vance to seek clarification of certain aspects of aircraft attrition. Detailed replies subsequently were incorporated into a JCS paper in which the service chiefs also cited two major policy handicaps of the air war that contributed to aircraft losses. These were the administration's restrictive targeting policies and its observance of the sanctuary areas around

Hanoi, Haiphong, and in the buffer zone adjacent to China. They endorsed the Hise Report finding that North Vietnam's air defense system eventually could make air attacks unprofitable and reaffirmed the need for more ECM equipment and suitable ordnance. They disagreed with the report's belief that pilot fatigue contributed to losses, but conceded some pilots had been overworked because occasionally there were insufficient numbers of them. They pointed to Admiral Sharp's recent directive (of 2 October) stating that sorties allocated for North Vietnam and Laos were not mandatory figures to be achieved but were issued to indicate the weight of air effort that should go into certain areas. Air units were not to be pressed beyond a reasonable point.[20]

McNamara's Proposal to Reduce Aircraft Attrition

Meanwhile, based on a study by his Southeast Asia Program Division of 1965 aircraft loss rates, Secretary McNamara on 17 September sent the JCS a plan to reduce aircraft losses, particularly the Navy's. It took into consideration the Air Force's force structure which the division believed could absorb aircraft losses more easily. To reduce Navy losses, the Defense Secretary suggested shifting about 1,000 carrier sorties per month from North Vietnam and Laos to South Vietnam with the Air Force increasing its sortie activities in those two countries. He thought this might reduce Navy losses by about 59 aircraft during the next nine months. In absolute numbers, USAF losses had been less and Navy losses more than planned, in part because some "higher loss" targets initially planned for the Air Force had been assigned to the Navy. Loss rates varied widely by target. Overall, Mr. McNamara saw no significant difference in the air performance of the two services, asserting that "I think they're both doing a magnificent job and I see no difference as measured by loss rates in their effectiveness in combat." [21]

Generals McConnell and Harris strongly opposed any change in sortie assignments. So did the JCS which on 6 October replied by noting that differences between projected and actual aircraft losses in December 1965 had stemmed primarily from the high level of air effort in route packages V and VIA and the significant increase in enemy air defenses. The Joint Chiefs also observed that OSD had underestimated both total combat sorties to be flown over North Vietnam and Navy's noncombat aircraft losses. A shift in sorties to reduce losses would pose considerable operational difficulties for the Air Force by requiring more flying time and air refueling missions in order to reach the northernmost targets. The Navy too would have to make important operational adjustments. [22]

Affirming that every effort was being made to reduce aircraft and aircrew losses, the JCS again recommended Rolling Thunder program 52 as the best solution. It also noted that, under current projections, even with the recently announced (22 September)* procurement increase, new production would not equal aircraft losses. [23]

In view of this reply, Secretary McNamara abandoned plans to switch Air Force and Navy operational areas.

---

* See p 52.

V. THE AIR WAR AT YEAR'S END

While the Air Force concentrated on Tally-Ho strikes, the administration in late 1966 took another look at JCS proposals to increase the air pressure on North Vietnam. During a conference in October in Honolulu to review additional U.S. force deployments, Admiral Sharp proposed a revised strike program averaging 11,100 sorties per month against the North for 18 months beginning in January 1967. On 4 November the JCS endorsed both the deployment and sortie proposals and again advocated mining the sea approaches to North Vietnam's principal ports, as well as several other actions.[1]

On 8 November General Wheeler urged Secretary McNamara to approve the Rolling Thunder program 52 sent to him initially on 22 August. Except for some fixed targets, the program would prohibit armed reconnaissance within a 10-nautical-mile radius of Hanoi and Phuc Yen airfield and the Haiphong sanctuary would be limited to a radius of four nautical miles. The JCS chairman singled out a number of other major targets remaining in the North, commenting briefly on each. He proposed striking three SA-2 supply sites, observing that since 1 July 1965 at least 949 SA-2's had been launched against U.S. aircraft, destroying 32. He suggested attacks on certain POL storage facilities, estimating that 24,800 metric tons remained of an initial 132,000 metric tons of fixed POL storage capacity. Dispersed sites, he said, held about 42,500 metric tons. Other targets on his list included the Thai Nguyen steel plant, the Haiphong cement plant, two Haiphong power plants, four waterway locks (related to water transportation), and the port areas of Cam Pha and Haiphong.[2]

On 10 November Secretary Brown informed Secretary McNamara that he endorsed the proposed Rolling Thunder 52 program. It would include 472 strike sorties against selective targets (canal water locks, POL storage areas, manufacturing and electric power plants, and SA-2 support facilities) in route package areas V, VIA, and VIB. On the basis of 1 April - 30 September 1966 attrition rates, there would be a loss of eight aircraft. He thought the air strikes would reduce and discourage shipping operations, reduce POL storage, increase replenishment, repair, and construction problems, and make more difficult the resupply of Communist forces in the South.[3]

Approval of Rolling Thunder Program 52

The administration on 12 November approved a modified Rolling Thunder program 52. It contained 13 previously unauthorized JCS targets: a bridge, a railroad yard, a cement plant and two power plants in Haiphong, two POL facilities, two SA-2 supply sites, and selected elements of the Thai Nguyen steel plant. Ten vehicle depots also were earmarked for attack. To assure success of the overall program, the JCS raised the authorized attack sortie level to 13,200 per month for November. In separate but related planning action, Secretary McNamara limited the JCS-recommended air and ground deployment program through June 1968 on the grounds that an excessively large buildup could jeopardize some recently achieved economic stability in South Vietnam.[4]

Despite the new attack sortie authorization, the northeast monsoons restricted program "52" operations for the remainder of 1966. Actual sorties flown in November totaled 7,252 (3,681 USAF) and in December, 6,732 (USAF 4,129). These figures compared with the year's high of 12,154

U.S. attack sorties flown against the North in September. A sudden administration decision in November to defer striking six of the approved JCS targets also affected the sortie rate.[5]

Among the authorized targets were the Hai Gai POL storage site, hit on 22 November by USAF F-4C's, and the Dap Cai railroad bridge, a holdover from program "51". Navy aircraft struck the Haiphong SA-2 supply complex and the Cam Thon POL storage area. On 2 December USAF aircraft hit the Hoa Gai site for a second time while Navy aircraft conducted a first strike against the Van Vien vehicle depot. The latter was subsequently hit six times through 14 December. USAF aircraft also hit Yen Vien railroad YARD year for the first time twice on 4 December and conducted restrikes on 13 and 14 December. Both the vehicle depot and the railroad yard were heavily damaged.[6]

The Furor Over Air Strikes "On Hanoi"

The USAF and Navy strikes of 13 and 14 December against the Van Vien vehicle depot and the Yen Vien railroad yard had international repercussions. The depot was about five nautical miles south of Hanoi and the yard, a major junction of three rail lines with two of them connecting with China, about six nautical miles northeast of Hanoi. Both the North Vietnamese and Russians immediately charged that aircraft had struck residential areas of Hanoi, killing or wounding 100 civilians. Allegedly, several foreign embassies were also hit, including Communist China's. Headquarters MACV quickly asserted that only military targets were struck. The State Department conceded that the attacking aircraft might have accidentally hit residential areas but strongly suggested that Hanoi's antiaircraft fire and SA-2 missiles (of which more than 100 were fired during the two days, a record high) may have caused the civilian damage.[7]

Debriefings of the crews of seven USAF flights participating in the 13 and 14 December strikes on the railroad yard indicated that two flights experienced problems. The crews of one had difficulty acquiring the target and were uncertain of the exact release coordinates because of clouds and a MIG attack. Although they thought the ordnance was released in the immediate target area, they conceded it might have fallen slightly southwest of a bridge located south of the railroad yard. Poor weather also prevented the crews of a second flight from seeing the railroad yard and bomb impact was not observed, although they thought the ordnance struck rolling stock.[8]

The Communist allegations -- and the growing criticism by certain groups in the United States and abroad about the war's escalation -- prompted the administration on 16 December to suspend further attacks on the Yen Vien railroad yard. On the 23d Admiral Sharp advised all subordinate commands that until further notice no air attacks were authorized within 10 nautical miles of the center of Hanoi. Attacks on other fixed targets were also halted for the time being. On 26 December a New York Times correspondent, Harrison E. Salisbury, who arrived in Hanoi on the 23d reported on alleged eyewitness accounts of the 13 and 14 December air strikes that resulted in civilian casualties and damage. The Defense Department on the same day acknowledged that some civilian areas may have been struck accidentally but reemphasized its policy to bomb only military targets in the North and to take all possible care to avoid civilian casualties. It was impossible, it said, to avoid some damage to civilian areas.[9]

Other Air Operations in November and December

Other air action in the last two months of 1966 included restrikes along the Hanoi-Lai Cai railroad line in route package V and continuation of the Tally-Ho air campaign in route package I. In fact, about 43 percent of the total U.S. air effort in the North -- and 64 percent of the USAF effort -- was directed against targets in route package I. An Air Force compilation of the results of the Tally-Ho air campaign from 20 July through November showed the following:

	Destroyed	Damaged	Other
Trucks	72	61	
Structures	1,208	624	
Watercraft	85	132	
Antiaircraft and air warning positions	92	22	
Roads cut, cratered, or seeded			339
Landslides			6
Secondary explosions			1,414

Nevertheless there was still considerable uncertainty as to the overall effect of this air program on North Vietnam's ability to resupply the South.[10]

A limited number of USAF road cutting and other air strikes were also made in route packages II, III, and IV. There were no B-52 strikes in the North in November but in December 78 sorties were flown in the DMZ and 35 sorties slightly above the zone. From 12 April 1966 when the first strike was conducted against North Vietnam through the end of the year, B-52's flew 280 sorties including 104 sorties in "DMZ North." The major B-52 effort was directed against targets in South Vietnam. Year-end operations were also highlighted by 48-hour Christmas and New Year "truces". Although bombing ceased over the North during each truce period, USAF reconnaissance flights continued. USAF attack sorties for the year totaled 44,500 -- slightly more than 54 percent of the 81,948 attack sorties flown in the North by all U.S. and VNAF aircraft.[11]

Meanwhile, the JCS in November asked Admiral Sharp to comment on the "Combat Beaver" proposal that the Air Staff had developed in conjunction with the other services to support Secretary McNamara's proposed electronic and ground barrier between North and South Vietnam. Using Steel Tiger, Gate Guard, and Tally-Ho experience, Combat Beaver called for day and night air strikes on key logistic centers. This, it was hoped, would create new concentrations of backed-up enemy materiel and equipment suitable for air strikes. It would complement any ground barrier system and could begin immediately.[12]

Admiral Sharp's comments were critical. He said that with certain exceptions Combat Beaver was similar to the current air program. He thought that it overstressed the importance of air strikes in route packages II, III, and IV and would result in high aircraft losses. It would not, in his view, increase overall air effectiveness but, instead, disrupt the existing well-balanced air effort. Taking into account CINCPAC's comments and those of other agencies, the Air Staff reworked the proposal and, at the end of December, produced a new one, designating it the integrated strike and interdiction plan (ISIP).[13]

Assessment of Enemy Air Defenses

By the end of 1966 the overwhelming number of U.S. combat aircraft losses in the North was still caused by conventional antiaircraft fire. The Seventh Air Force estimated the enemy's antiaircraft strength

CHRONOLOGY OF THE GROWTH OF NORTH VIETNAM'S
AIR DEFENSES
1964-1966

Jul 64	Air defense system based on obsolescent equipment. Antiaircraft guns, 50; SA-2's, 0; air defense radars, 24; fighter aircraft, 0.
Aug 64	Introduction of MIG-15's.
Mar 65	Introduction of improved air defense radars such as ground control intercept.
Apr 65	First use of MIG fighter aircraft. Detection of first SA-2 site under construction.
Jun 65	Increase in air defense radars to 41.
Jul 65	First SA-2 fired at U.S. aircraft. Introduction of 100mm antiaircraft guns.
Aug 65	Significant increase in low-altitude air defense radar coverage. Increase in antiaircraft strength to about 3,000 guns.
Dec 65	Introduction of MIG-21's. Beginning of emission control of air defense radar.
Mar 66	Introduction of system for identification, friend or foe.
Jul 66	First MIG use of air-to-air missiles.
Aug 66	Completion of a sophisticated air defense system. Antiaircraft guns, 4,400; SA-2's, 20 to 25 firing battalions; air defense radars, 271; fighter aircraft, 65.
Dec 66	Air defense system includes: light and medium antiaircraft guns, 6,398; SA-2 sites, 151; SA-2 firing battalions, 25; MIG-15's and -17's, 32; MIG-21's, 15; use of air-to-air missile

SOURCE: Briefing Rprt on Factors Affecting A/C Losses in SEA, 26 Sep 66, prepared by Col. H.W. Hise, JCS (TS); USAF Mgt Summary (S), 6 Jan 67; p 70; Ops Review Gp, Dir/Ops, Hq USAF; <u>N.Y. Times</u>, Jul 66.

had grown from 5,000 to 7,400 guns during the year. Nevertheless, U.S. aircraft losses were decreasing with 17 downed in November and 20 in December. The Air Force lost 24 -- 12 in each of the two months.[14]

The MIG threat increased in December, apparently in response to the latest U.S. attacks on important targets. During 35 encounters and 16 engagements two F-105's were lost as against one MIG. One of the losses, on 14 December, was the first one attributed to a MIG-21 air-to-air missile. Other air-to-air missiles were fired on at least five occasions during the month, but U.S. air superiority was easily maintained. Between 3 April 1965, when the MIG's first entered the war, and 31 December 1966 there were a total of 179 encounters and 93 engagements. The aerial battles cost the enemy 28 MIG's as against 9 U.S. aircraft, a ratio of 1 to 2.8. Of the nine losses, seven were USAF and two were Navy. In addition, there were two "probable" USAF losses to MIG's. In December, the enemy's combat aircraft inventory, recently augmented by Soviet deliveries, was believed to consist of 32 MIG-15's and -17's, 15 MIG-21's, and six IL-28's, all at Phuc Yen airfield.[15]

SA-2's continued to take a small but steady toll. They claimed one USAF aircraft in November and three in December. Because the missiles precluded the use of optimum air tactics, Admiral Sharp on 22 November proposed to the JCS a major effort to solve the SA-2 problem. He placed the current SA-2 strength at 28 to 32 firing battalions[+] and warned that the number would increase unless air restrictions were eased. Already a shortage of special munitions and properly equipped aircraft prevented a

---

* See p 64 and app 8.

+ The year-end estimate was 25 battalions. See p 64.

large-scale attack on these mobile, well-camouflaged units. Only a "blitzkrieg" type of attack could prevent their movement.[16]

For the short term, Admiral Sharp recommended the use of all available aircraft to detect SA-2 sites, revision of the current targeting system to include SA-2 assembly and storage areas regardless of location, a priority intelligence effort to locate key SA-2 control facilities, and attacks on high priority targets in the North in random fashion to avoid establishing a predictable pattern of attack. He also urged steps to increase Shrike production, assure positive control and tracking of all U.S. aircraft through the USAF "Big Eye" EC-121 program, improve distribution of SA-2 data, exploit more fully color photography in penetrating camouflage, and equip all aircraft with ECM, chaff, homing radars, and warning receivers. Further, the State and Defense Departments should release statements to discourage the Soviets from deploying additional SA-2 systems by pointing to the danger of escalation, and the "intelligence community" should constantly review and distribute all relevant SA-2 information.

For the long term, Admiral Sharp said there was a need to expedite procurement of an antiradiation missile, develop better warheads using the implosion principle, employ beacons to aid in finding SA-2 emitters, provide VHF/UHF homing capabilities for Wild Weasel aircraft, and improve data exchange between the Rome Air Development Center and Southeast Asia operational activities.[17]

The Air Staff generally agreed with Admiral Sharp's recommendations. The JCS also concurred and directed General McConnell to procure and deploy adequate numbers of anti-SA-2 devices and equipment. The Joint Chiefs were still undecided at the end of the year whether to recommend to Secretary McNamara an all-out campaign against the SA-2's in the immediate future.[18]

Assessments of the Air War Against North Vietnam

As 1966 ended, General McConnell and the Air Staff remained convinced that greater use of air power, especially in North Vietnam, was the only alternative to a long, costly war of attrition. They also thought it would make unnecessary the massive buildup of U.S. and allied ground forces still under way. Although the combined air and ground effort in Southeast Asia had prevented a Communist takeover of South Vietnam, one Air Staff assessment found no significant trend toward the attainment of other U.S. objectives in that country.[19]

Within the JCS General McConnell continued to support recommendations to reduce operational restrictions and expand target coverage in the North. The level of air effort was less than he desired, but he believed air power had shown how it could be tailored to the geography of a country and, by the selection of weapons and mode of air attack, be responsive to political and psychological considerations. In some instances, it was clear, the Vietnam experience ran counter to conventional air power concepts. As he had observed in May, "tactical bombing" in South Vietnam was being conducted in part by "strategic" B-52 bombers and "strategic" bombing of the North was being conducted largely by "tactical bombers".[20]

(U) Any evaluation of the effect of air power, especially in the North, had to consider political factors which limited military activity. To deal with this circumstance, General McConnell offered the following dictum: "Since air power, like our other military forces, serves a political objective, it is also subject to political restraints. Therefore, we must qualify any assessments of air power's effectiveness on the basis of limitations that govern its application."[21]

General Harris, the PACAF commander, singled out three principal factors hampering the air campaign against North Vietnam: political restraints and geographical sanctuaries that precluded striking more lucrative targets, poor weather for prolonged periods of time, and Hanoi's ability to repair and reconstruct damaged target areas. With respect to the last, PACAF officials acknowledged the North Vietnamese had "exceptional" recuperative capabilities to counter air attacks on trucks, rolling stock, and the lines of communications. They had built road and rail by-passes and bridges in minimum time, dispersed POL by using pack animals, human porters and watercraft, and developed an effective air defense system. Infiltration through the DMZ, Laos, and Cambodia was placed at 7,000 to 9,000 men per month,* and the enemy logistic system was supporting an estimated 128,000 combat and combat support personnel with out-of-country resources. General Harris thought that an important "lesson learned" was that the gradual, drawn-out air campaign had created very little psychological impact on Hanoi's leaders and the populace. He also continued to believe (as did the Air Staff and other Air Force commanders in Southeast Asia) that control of air operations in the North -- as well as in Laos and South Vietnam -- was too fragmented and should be centralized under a single air commander.[22]

Admiral Sharp's view of the air campaign against the North in 1966 was that little had been accomplished in preventing external assistance to the enemy. Except for the June strikes on POL targets in Haiphong

---

* MACV and DIA eventually estimated that about 81,000 North Vietnamese tered South Vietnam in 1966. The infiltration rate was high in the first half and dropped sharply in the second half of the year.

(which handled 85 percent of the North's imports during the year), the port was almost undisturbed. Of the nearly 82,000 attack sorties flown during the year, less than one percent were against JCS-proposed targets. In the critical northeast area (route packages VIA and VIB), of 104 targets only 19 were hit in 1965 and 20 in 1966; the remaining 99 percent of attack sorties were armed reconnaissance and flown to harass, disrupt, and impede the movement of men and supplies on thousands of miles of roads, trails, and inland and coastal waterways. He noted that despite severe losses of vehicles, rolling stock, watercraft, supplies and men from air attack, the North Vietnamese were ingenious in hiding and dispersing their supplies and showed "remarkable" recuperative ability. He concluded that the overall amount of supplies and men moving through the DMZ, Laos, and Cambodia into South Vietnam probably was greater in 1966 than in 1965.[23]

(U) Secretary Brown took a somewhat different view of the air campaign believing it had inflicted "serious" logistic losses on the North. From 2 March 1965 (when the Rolling Thunder program began) through September 1966, air strikes had destroyed or damaged more than 7,000 trucks, 3,000 railway cars, 5,000 bridges, 15,000 barges and boats, two-thirds of the POL storage capacity, and many ammunition sites and other facilities. He cited prisoner of war reports indicating that troops in the South received no more than 50 percent of daily supply requirements.* In addition, the air war had diverted 200,000 to 300,000 personnel to road, rail, and bridge repair work, and combat troops for air defense.+ By December, military action in both North and South Vietnam had reduced battalion size attacks from seven

---

* See p 8.

\+ On 1 March 1967, Secretary McNamara estimated that Hanoi was using 125,000 men for its air defenses and "tens of thousands" of others for coastal defense.

to two per month and, in the past eight months, raised enemy casualties from 3,600 to 5,200 per month.

(U) Although infiltration from the North continued, Secretary Brown said: "I do not believe that an air blockade of land and sea routes will ever be completely effective any more than a sea blockade can prevent all commerce from entering or leaving a country." He thought the air attacks were becoming more effective due to improvements in intelligence, tactics, equipment, and techniques.

(U) The Air Force Secretary defended the administration's policy of exempting certain targets from air attack if they supported only the North's civilian economy, were close to urban areas and would cause civilian suffering if hit, and would not significantly affect in the short term the enemy's ability to continue fighting. He listed five criteria for judging whether to strike a target: its effect on infiltration from North to South, the extent of air defenses and possible U.S. aircraft losses, the degree of "penalty" inflicted on North Vietnam, the possibility of civilian casualties, and the danger of Soviet or Chinese intervention resulting in a larger war. He thought that a "Korean-type" victory -- with the aggressor pushed back and shown that aggression did not pay -- would meet U.S. objectives and make the war in Vietnam a "success." [24]

Secretary McNamara's views on the controlled use of air power against the North were well known. In a "deployment issue" paper sent to the JCS on 6 October in conjunction with deployment planning, he said that intelligence reports and aerial reconnaissance clearly showed how the air program against the North effectively harassed and delayed truck movements and materiel into the South but had no effect on troop infiltration moving along trails. He thought that the cost to the enemy to replace trucks and cargo as a result of stepped up air strikes would be negligible compared with the cost of greatly increased U.S. aircraft losses. In a summation of his views on the war before House Subcommittees in February 1967 he further stated:

> For those who thought that air attacks on North Vietnam would end the aggression in South Vietnam, the results from this phase of the operations have been disappointing. But for those who understood the political and economic structure of North Vietnam, the results have been satisfactory. Most of the war materiel sent from North Vietnam to South Vietnam is provided by other Communist countries and no amount of destruction of the industrial capacity . . . can, by itself, eliminate this flow . . . .

When the bombing campaign began he added, "we did not believe that air attacks on North Vietnam, by themselves, would bring its leaders to the conference table or break the morale of its people -- and they have not done so."

(U) The Defense Secretary also observed that although air strikes had destroyed two-thirds of their POL storage capacity, the North Vietnamese had continued to bring it in "over the beach" and disperse it. POL shortages did not appear to have greatly impeded the North's war effort. He reiterated the U.S. policy that "the bombing of the North is intended as a supplement to and not a substitute for the military operations in the South."[25]

NOTES

Chapter I

1. Hist (TS), CINCPAC, 1965, vol II, pp 326 and 328; Project CHECO SEA Rprt (TS), 15 Dec 66, subj: Comd and Control, 1965, pp 1-7; memo (TS), Lt Col B.F. Echols, Exec, Dir/Plans to AFCHO, 27 Nov 67, subj: Review of Draft Hist Study, "The Air Campaign Against NVN."

2. Hist (TS), CINCPAC, 1965, vol II, pp 326 and 328; Testimony of Gen J.P. McConnell, CSAF on 9 May 66 before Senate Preparedness Investigating Subcmte of Cmte on Armed Services, 89th Cong, 2d Sess (U) 9-10 May 66, USAF Tactical Air Ops and Readiness, pp 25-26.

3. Rprt (TS), An Eval of the Effects of the Air Campaign Against NVN and Laos, prepared by Jt Staff, Nov 66, in Dir/Plans; Talking Paper for the JCS for the State-JCS Mtg on 1 Apr 66 (TS), Undated, subj: Discussions with Mr. Bundy on Far Eastern Matters, in Dir/Plans; Hist (TS), CINCPAC, 1965, vol II, pp 339-41; memo (TS), Col D.G. Gravenstine, Chief Ops Review Gp, Dir/Ops to AFCHO, 22 Nov 67, subj: Draft of AFCHO Hist Study.

4. Memo (TS), Col J.C. Berger, Asst Dir for Jt Matters, Dir/Ops to CSAF, 10 Aug 66; Background Paper on Division of R/T Area (TS), Mar 66, both in Dir/Plans; Excerpts from Gen Moore's Presentation to the JCS (TS), 13 Jul 66, in OSAF; Project CHECO SEA Rprts (TS), 15 Dec 66, subj: Comd and Control, 1965, pp 1-9; and 1 Mar 67, subj: Control of Air Strikes in SEA, pp 95-97; memo (TS), Echols to AFCHO, 27 Nov 67.

5. Van Staaveren (TS), 1965, pp 71-74; N.Y. Times, 1 Feb 66.

6. Memo (TS), Col J.H. Germeraad, Asst Dep Dir of Plans for War Plans, Dir/Plans to CSAF, 10 Jan 66, subj: Strat for SEA; Background Paper on Pertinent Testimony by SECDEF and JCS given on 20 Jan 66 (TS), 20 Jan 66, both in Dir/Plans.

7. JCSM-16-66 (TS), 8 Jan 66.

8. Memo (TS), Lt Gen J.T. Carroll, Dir DIA to SECDEF, 21 Jan 66, subj: An Appraisal of the Bombing of NVN, in Dir/Plans; JCSM-41-66 (TS), 18 Jan 66.

9. JCSM-56-66 (TS), 25 Jan 66.

10. JCS 2343/751 (TS), 13 Jan 66; SM-82-66 (TS), 22 Jan 66.

11. Memo (TS), SECDEF to Chmn JCS, 5 Jan 66, no subj: in Dir/Plans; CM-1135-66 (TS), 22 Jan 66.

12. Testimony of Secy McNamara on 26 Jan 66 before House Subcmte on Appns, 89th Cong, 2d Sess (U), <u>Supplemental Def Appns for 1966</u>, p 31.

13. Ibid., p 32; background briefing by U.S. officials (U), 31 Jan 66, in SAFOI.

14. Memo (TS), SECDEF to Pres, 24 Jan 66, subj: The Mil Outlook in SVN, in Dir/Plans; Hist (TS), CINCPAC, 1966, vol II, p 605.

15. <u>Wash Post,</u> 1 Feb 66; <u>N.Y. Times,</u> 1 Feb 66.

16. Intvw (U), McConnell with Hearst Panel, 21 Mar 66, in SAFOI; Hist (TS), CINCPAC, 1966, vol II, p 491; Rprt (TS), Dir/Ops, 20 Apr 66, subj: SEA Counter-Air Alternatives, p A-28, in AFCHO.

17. Memo (TS), Col D.G. Cooper, Ofc Dep Dir of Plans for War Plans, Dir/Plans to CSAF, 12 Feb 66, subj: The Employment of Air Power in the War in NVN; Briefing of JCS R/T Study Gp Rprt (TS), 6 Apr 66, subj: Air Ops Against NVN, App A; Rprt (TS), An Eval of Effect of the Air Campaign Against NVN and Laos, all in Dir/Plans; Hist (TS), CINCPAC, 1966, vol II, pp 493-44; Jacob Van Staaveren, <u>USAF Deployment Planning for SEA</u> (AFCHO, 1966) (TS), pp 1-2 and 26 (hereinafter cited as Van Staaveren, 1966).

18. CM-1147-66 (TS), 1 Feb 66.

19. Hist (TS), CINCPAC, 1966, vol II, pp 510-11; Van Staaveren (TS), 1966, ch II.

20. Memo (U), Lt Gen H.T. Wheless, Asst Vice CSAF to Deps, Dirs, Chiefs of Comparable Ofces, 17 Feb 66, subj: Analysis of Air Power, in Dir/Plans; Van Staaveren, 1966, pp 10-15.

21. Memo (S), Lt Gen R.R. Compton, DCS/P&O to DCS/P&R, 21 Feb 66, subj: Organization in SEA, in Dir/Plans.

22. Memo (TS), Maj Gen S.J. McKee, Asst DCS/Plans and Ops for JCS to CSAF, 18 Feb 66, subj: Air Ops Against NVN; JCSM-113-66 (TS), 19 Feb 66, both in Dir/Plans.

23. Testimony of Secy McNamara on 25 Jan 66 before House Subcmte on Appns, 89th Cong, 2d Sess (U), <u>Supplementary Def Appns for 1966</u>, pp 33 and 39; memo (TS), Cooper to CSAF, 12 Feb 66, subj: The Employment of Air Power in the War in VN; memo (TS), McKee to SECDEF, 24 Mar 66, subj: Air Ops against NVN, both in Dir/Plans; <u>N.Y. Times,</u> 5 Feb 66.

Chapter II

1. Jacob Van Staaveren, <u>USAF Plans and Operations in Southeast Asia</u> (AFCHO, 1965) (TS), p 50 (hereinafter cited as Van Staaveren, 1965); Van Staaveren, 1966, pp 4 and 19.

2. Rprt (S), SEA Air Ops, Mar 66, pp 2-3, prepared by Dir/Tac Eval, Hqs PACAF (hereinafter cited as PACAF rprt); JCS R/T Study Gp Rprt (TS), 6 Apr 67, App A; ltr (TS), CINCPAC to JCS, 18 Sep, subj: An Eval of CY 66-67 Force Rqmts; rprt (TS), Eval of Effects of the Air Campaign Against NVN and Laos, Nov 66, all in Dir/Plans; JCSM-153-66 (TS), 10 Mar 66.

3. Memo (TS), McKee to Gen. W. H. Blanchard, Vice CSAF, 23 Mar 66, subj: Air Ops Against Aflds in NVN, in Dir/Ops; Hist (TS) MACV, 1966, p 431; Hist (TS), CINCPAC, 1966, Vol II, p 494.

4. Memo (TS), McKee to CSAF, 25 Mar 66, subj: Acft Losses Over NVN, w/atch Talking Paper, in Dir/Plans; intvw (U), McConnell with Hearst Panel, 21 Mar 66 in SAFOI; rprt (TS),Dir/Plans, 20 Apr 66, p A-34; N.Y. Journal American, 20 Mar 66.

5. Hist (S), Dir/Ops, Jul-Dec 66, p 10; Hq USAF Ops Analysis Initial Progress Rprt (S), Mar 66, subj: Analysis of Effectiveness of Interdiction in SEA, in AFCHO.

6. Hq USAF Ops Analysis Second Progress Rprt (S), May 66, subj: Analysis of Effectiveness of Air Interdiction in SEA, ch V, in AFCHO.

7. Summary of Action by JCS (TS), 25 Mar 66, subj: Air Ops Against NVN, in Dir/Plans; Hist (TS), CINCPAC, 1966, vol II, p 497.

8. CSAFM-W-66 (TS), 20 Jan 66; CSAFM-P-23-66 and CMCM-33-66 (TS), 18 Apr 66; Talking Paper on Air Interdiction NVN/Laos (TS), 6 Jul 66; rprt (TS), An Eval of the Effects of the Air Campaign Against NVN and Laos, Nov 66, all in Dir/Plans; Hist (TS), CINCPAC, 1966, vol II, p 497; Hist (TS), MACV 1966, p 431.

9. CSAFM-W-66 (TS), 20 Jun 66; rprt (TS), An Eval of the Effects of the Air Campaign Against NVN and Laos, Nov 66, PACAF rprt (S), SEA Air Ops, Apr 66, pp 3-8, all in Dir/Plans.

10. DAF Order No 559N (U), 26 Mar 66, in AFCHO; Hist (TS), CINCPAC, 1966, vol II, p 468; tel to Ofc of Asst for Gen Officer Matters, DCS/P (U), 15 Aug 67.

11. PACAF rprt (S), SEA Air Ops, Apr 66, p 388, in Dir/Ops; Seventh AF Chronology, 1 Jul 65-30 Jun 66 (S), p 48; Hq USAF Ops Analysis Second Progress Rprt (S), May 66, pp 39-44, both in AFCHO; Project CHECO SEA Rprts (TS), 15 Jul 67, subj: R/T, Jul 65-Dec 66, p 50, and 21 Jul 67, subj: Expansion of USAF Ops in SEA, 1966, pp 100-03; Hist (TS), CINCPAC, 1966, vol II, p 575.

12. Seventh AF Chronology, 1 Jul 65-30 Jun 66, p 51; PACAF rprt (S), SEA Air Ops, Apr 66, pp 3-8.

13. Background Paper on the Division of the R/T Area (TS), Mar 66; Talking Paper on the Division of the R/T Area (TS), Mar 66, both in Dir/Plans; Hist (TS), CINCPAC, 1966, vol II, pp 494-95.

14. Memo (TS), McKee to CSAF, 16 Apr 66, subj: Priority of Air Effort in SEA; memo (TS), SECDEF to Chmn JCS, 14 Apr 66, no subj: ltr (TS), CINCPAC to JCS, 18 Sep 66, subj: Eval of CY 66-67 Force Rqmts w/atch MACV Rprt (TS), 5 Sep 66; CM-1354-66 (TS), 20 Apr 66; Background Paper on R/T Areas (TS), Mar 66, all in Dir/Plans; Hist (TS), CINCPAC, 1966, vol II, pp 494-97; memo (TS), Gravenstine to AFCHO, 22 Nov 67.

15. JCS 2343/805-1 (TS), 14 Apr 66.

16. CSAFM-P-30-66 (TS), 20 Apr 66; memo (TS), Maj Gen L. D. Clay, Dep Dir of Plans to CSAF, 26 Jul 66, subj: U.S. Strat for SEA and S.W. Pacific; JCS 2343/805-1 (TS), 14 Apr 66; JCS 2343/805-5, 22 Jul 66, all in Dir/Plans.

17. JCS R/T Study Gp Rprt (TS), 6 Apr 66, subj: Air Ops Against NVN; memo (TS), McKee to CSAF, 13 Apr 66, subj: R/T Study Gp Rprt, Air Ops Against NVN; memo (TS), Gravenstine to AFCHO, 22 Nov 66.

18. CSAFM-P-22-66 (TS), 13 Apr 66; memo (TS), McKee to CSAF, 13 Apr 66; JCSM-238-66 (TS), 14 Apr 66, all in Dir/Plans.

19. Transcript (U), Secy Brown's remarks on "Meet the Press," 22 May 66, in SAFOI.

20. Memo (S), Berger to CSAF, 15 Sep 66, subj: 7th AF Ops in RP II, III, and IV; PACAF rprt (S), SEA Air Ops, May 66, pp 1-8, both in Dir/Plans.

21. PACAF rprt (S), SEA Air Ops, May 66, pp 1-8; Seventh AF Chronology, 1 Jul 65 to 30 Jun 66, p 52; ltr (TS), CINCPAC to JCS, 18 Sep 66; Project CHECO SEA Rprts (TS), 9 Sep 66, subj: Night Interdiction in SEA, pp 33-37, and 25 May 67, subj: Interdiction in SEA (1965-1966), pp 39-69.

22. Testimony of McConnell on 9 May 66 before Senate Preparedness Investigating Subcmte (TS), pp 16-17 (AFCHO's classified copy); PACAF rprt (S), SEA Air Ops, May 66, pp 1-8 and 22; CINCPACFLT Analysis Staff Study 9-66 (TS), 12 Jul 66, subj: Combat Effectiveness of the SA-2 through Mid-1966, both in Dir/Plans.

23. Memo (S), Maj Gen R. N. Smith, Dir of Plans to DCS/P&O, 3 May 66, subj: Capabilities for Aerial Blockade; msg 87716 (TS), CSAF to SAC, PACAF, TAC, USAFE, 6 May 66, both in Dir/Plans.

24. Msg 95413 (TS), CINCPACAF to CSAF, 24 May 66, in Dir/Plans.

25. Hist (S), Dir/Ops, Jul-Dec 66, p 126; PACAF rprt (S), SEA Air Ops, Jun 66, pp 6-9; Seventh AF Chronology, 1 Jul 65-30 Jun 66, (S), p 52; ltr (TS), CINCPAC to JCS, 18 Sep 66; Project CHECO SEA Rprt (S), 9 Aug 67, subj: Combat Skyspot, pp 6 and 19; Project CHECO SEA Rprt (TS), 9 Sep 66, subj: Night Interdiction in SEA, pp 33-37.

26. PACAF rprt (S), SEA Air Ops, Jun 66, pp 6-9; Project CHECO SEA Rprt (TS), 9 Sep 66, subj: Night Interdiction in SEA, pp 33-37.

27. Project CHECO SEA Rprt (TS), 25 May 67, subj: Interdiction in SEA, 1965-1966, pp 60-61.

Chapter III

1. Memo (TS), R. Helms, Acting Dir CIA to Dep SECDEF, 27 Dec 65, subj: Probable Reaction to U.S. Bombing of POL Targets in NVN, in Dir/Plans.

2. Memo (TS), McKee to SECDEF, 24 Mar 66, subj: Air Ops Against NVN; memo (S), C.R. Vance, Dep SECDEF to Chmn JCS, 25 Apr 66, same subj; memo (TS), W.W. Rostow, Spec Asst to Pres to Secys State and Def, 6 May 66, no subj, all in Dir/Plans; study (TS), 27 Oct 66, subj: Effectiveness of Air Strikes Against NVN, prepared by Sys Analysis Div, Dept of Navy, in OSAF.

3. Memo (TS), Smith to CSAF, 16 Jun 66, subj: NVN Strike Prog, in Dir/Plans; Hist (TS), CINCPAC, 1966, vol II, p 498.

4. Ibid.; Testimony of McConnell on 9 May 66 before Senate Preparedness Investigating Subcmte of the Cmte on Armed Services (U), p 27.

5. Project CHECO SEA Rprt (TS), 15 Jul 67, subj: R/T, Jul 65-Dec 66, p 59; N.Y. News, 24 Jun 66; Wash Post, 30 Jun 66, N.Y. Times, 1 Jul 66.

6. Hist (TS), CINCPAC, 1966, vol II, pp 499-500; Hist (TS), MACV 1966, p 431; Wash Post, 26 Jun 66; Balt Sun, 27 Jun 66.

7. Project CHECO SEA Rprt (TS), 15 Jul 67, subj: R/T, Jul 65-Dec 66, p 64; Hist (TS), CINCPAC, 1966, vol II, pp 499-500; Van Staaveren, 1966, p 42; N.Y. Times, 1 Jul 66.

8. Wash Post, 30 Jun 66.

9. N.Y. Times, 1 Jul 66; Van Staaveren, 1966, p 42.

10. Ltr (TS), CINCPAC to JCS, 4 Aug 66, subj: CINCPAC Briefing for SECDEF, 8 Jul 66; memo (TS), A. Enthoven, Asst SECDEF for Sys Analysis to Secys of Mil Depts et al, 12 Jul 66, subj: CINCPAC July 8, 1966 Briefing, both in Dir/Plans; Hist (TS), CINCPAC, 1966, vol II, pp 510-11.

11. Ltr (TS), CINCPAC to JCS, 4 Aug 66; memo (TS), Enthoven to Secys of Mil Depts et al, 12 Jul 66.

12. Van Staaveren, 1966, pp 42-53.

Notes to Pages 35 - 40   77

13. PACAF rprt (S), SEA Air Ops, Jul 66, pp 4-7; Rpt (TS), An Eval of the Effect of the Air Campaign Against NVN and Laos, Nov 66; ltr (TS), CINCPAC to JCS, 4 Aug 66.

14. Hist (S), Dir/Ops, Jul-Dec 66, pp 13 and 20-22.

15. Memo (TS), Berger to CSAF, 15 Sep 66; Excerpts from Gen Moore's Presentation to the JCS (TS), 13 Jul 66; PACAF rprt (S), SEA Air Ops, Jul 66, pp 4-7; memo (TS), Gravenstine to AFCHO, 22 Nov 67.

16. Talking Paper for JCS for Their Mtg with Adm Sharp at the JCS Mtg of 23 Sep 66 (TS), 22 Sep 66, in Dir/Plans; PACAF rprt (S), SEA Air Ops, Aug 66, pp 1-2; Hist (TS), CINCPAC, 1966, vol II, pp 500-02.

17. Memo (TS), M/Gen J.E. Thomas, Asst CS/I to SAF, 14 Oct 66, subj: PACAF Rprt on the NVN POL Situation, in Dir/Plans.

18. PACAF Rprts (S), SEA Air Ops, Jul 66, pp 4-5, Aug 66, pp 1-3; Sep 66, pp 4 and 8; and Oct 66, pp 10-11, all in Ops Review Gp, Dir/Ops.

19. Talking Paper for JCS for Their Mtg with Adm Sharp . . . on 23 Sep 66 (TS), 22 Sep 66; PACAF rprts (S), SEA Air Ops, Jul 66, pp 4-5 and 20; Aug 66, p 22; Sep 66, p 23; and Oct 66, p 23.

20. PACAF rprt (S), SEA Air Ops, Jul 66, pp 4-5 and 20; N.Y. Times, 8 Jul 66 and 9 Aug 66; Wash Star, 8 Aug 66; Balt Sun, 22 Sep 66.

21. Project CHECO SEA Rprt (TS), 9 Sep 66, subj: Night Interdiction in SEA, pp 37-38; ltr (TS), CINCPAC to JCS, 18 Sep 66; Hist (TS), MACV, 1966, p 434; N.Y. Times, 31 Jul 66.

22. Project CHECO SEA Rpts (TS), 9 Sep 66, subj: Night Interdiction in SEA, pp 37-38; 21 Nov 66, subj: Operation Tally-Ho, pp vi and 1-12; 15 Feb 67, subj: Air Ops in the DMZ Area, pp 35-42; and 15 May 67, subj: Air Interdiction in SEA, pp 61 and 64; briefing (TS), by Brig Gen C.M. Talbott, Dep Dir Tac Air Control Center, 7th AF for SECDEF et al (Saigon), 10 Oct 66, Doc No 13 in Project CHECO SEA Rprt, 15 Feb 67 pt II; PACAF rprt (S), SEA Air Ops, Jul 66, pp 7-8; Wash Star, 1 Aug 66.

23. Memo (TS), Rear Adm F.J. Bloui, Dir Fast East Region, OSD to Dir of Jt Staff, 1 Jun 66, subj: Air Ops in the DMZ; msg (TS), JCS to CINCPAC, 20 Jun 66, both in Dir/Plans; Hist (TS), MACV, 1966, pp 24-25.

24. PACAF rprt (S), SEA Air Ops, Aug 66, p 6; JCSM-603-66 (TS), 17 Sep 66; N.Y. Times, 31 Jul 66.

25. Memo (S), McConnell to Dep SECDEF, 25 Aug 66, no subj, in Dir/Plans; Hist (S), Dir/Ops, Jul 66, p 255; Project CHECO SEA Rprt (TS), 21 Nov 66, subj: Operation Tally-Ho, pp 17-25.

26. PACAF rprt (S), SEA Air Ops, Oct 66, p 2; Project CHECO SEA Rprt (TS), 15 Feb 67, subj: Air Ops in the DMZ area, pp 22, 26-28, 37, and 41.

27. Project CHECO SEA Rprt (TS), 25 May 67, subj: Air Interdiction in SEA, 1965-1966, pp 64-65.

28. Memo for record (S), by Lt Col L. F. Duggan, Exec Asst Ofc, Dir Jt Staff, 13 Oct 66, no subj; memo (TS), undated, subj: JCS Assessment of the Threat, both in Dir/Plans; Briefing (TS), by Brig Gen Talbott, 10 Oct 66; Project CHECO SEA Rprt (TS), 15 Feb 67, subj: Air Ops in the DMZ area, 1966, pp 24-25 and 51; PACAF rprt (S), SEA Air Ops, pp 1-7 and 17.

29. Memo (TS), Holloway to SAF, 19 Oct 66, subj: Results of Air Effort Upon Movement Through NVN/SVN DMZ During Aug 66, in Dir/Plans.

30. Project CHECO SEA Rprt (TS), 25 May 67, subj: Air Interdiction in SEA, 1965-1966, p 68; Doc 96 in Project CHECO SEA Rprt, 15 Feb 67, pt II.

Chapter IV

1. Hist (S), Dir/Ops, Jul-Dec 66, pp 20-23.

2. Memo (S), Col F.W. Vetter, Mil Asst to SAF to Vice CSAF, 3 Aug 66, subj: Significance of Watercraft Destroyed in NVN, in Dir/Plans.

3. *Ibid.*

4. Hist (S), Dir/Ops, Jul-Dec 66, pp 23-24; memo (TS), Gravenstine to AFCHO, 22 Nov 66.

5. Memo (TS), SECDEF to SAF, SN, 2 Sep 66, subj: Night Ops in SEA, in OSAF.

6. *Ibid.*

7. Memo (S), SN to SECDEF, 28 Sep 66, subj: Study Results: Night Ops in NVN, in OSAF.

8. Memo (S), SAF to SECDEF, 10 Nov 66, no subj; study (TS), 27 Oct 66, subj: Effectiveness of Air Strikes Against NVN.

9. Memo (TS), SN to SECDEF, 3 Nov 66, subj: Study of Effectiveness of Air Strikes Against NVN w/atch study (TS), 27 Oct 67, subj: Effectiveness of Air Strikes, both in OSAF; memo (TS), Gravenstine to AFCHO, 22 Nov 67.

10. Memo (TS), SAF to SECDEF, 10 Nov 66.

Notes to Pages 49 - 58

11. Memo (S), SAF to SECDEF, 19 Jul 66, subj: A/C Attrition in SEA, in Dir/Plans.

12. <u>Ibid.</u>

13. Memo (S), SAF to SECDEF, 24 Aug 66, subj: Questions Resulting from Briefing on Night Ops in SEA; memo (TS), McConnell to Dep SECDEF, 25 Aug 66, subj: JCS 2343/894-1, 25 Aug 66, both in OSAF.

14. Memo (S), Clay to CSAF, 25 Aug 66, subj: SEA Tac Ftr Attrition and A/C Proc Prog; memo (S), Holloway to Chmn JCS, 29 Aug 66, subj: SEA Tac Ftr Attrition and A/C Procur, both in Dir/Plans.

15. <u>N.Y. Times,</u> 23 Sep 66.

16. Briefing Rprt of Factors Affecting A/C Losses in SEA (S), 26 Sep 66, prepared by Col. H.W. Hise, Chmn, JCS A/C Losses Study Gp; JCS A/C Losses Study Gp Rprt (TS), Nov 66, subj: Factors Affecting Combat Air Ops and A/C Losses in SEA, both in Dir/Plans.

17. Msg 20135 (S), CINCPACAF to CSAF, 20 Oct 66, in OSAF; CINCPACFLT Analysis Staff Study 9-66 (TS), 12 Jul 66, subj: Combat Effectiveness of the SA-2 Through Mid-1966; Briefing Rprt of Factors Affecting A/C Losses in SEA (S), 26 Sep 66, both in Dir/Plans; Hist (S), Dir/Ops, Jul-Dec 66, pp 272-74.

18. Msg 20135 (S), CINCPACAF to CSAF, 20 Oct 66; Briefing Rprt of Factors Affecting A/C Losses in SEA (S), 26 Sep 66.

19. Memos (S), Clay to CSAF, 23 and 27 Sep and 3 Oct 66, same subjs: Factors Affecting A/C Losses in SEA, in Dir/Plans; JCSM-651-66, 10 Oct 66.

20. Memo (U), 22 Oct 66, subj: Secy Brown's Questions Concerning the Hise Rprt, in OSAF; Talking Paper for Chmn JCS on an Analysis of Air Ops in NVN to be discussed with SECDEF on 12 Nov 66 (TS), 11 Nov 66, subj: Analysis of Air Ops in NVN, both in Dir/Plans; JCS 2343/956-1 (TS), 15 Nov 66.

21. Memo (S), SECDEF to Chmn JCS, 17 Sep 66, subj: SEA Utilization of A/C, in OSAF; transcript (U), SECDEF News Briefing, 22 Sep 66, in SAFOI.

22. Memo (TS), Chief, PAC Div, Jt Staff to J-3, 17 Sep 66, subj: Utilization of A/C in SEA; in OSAF; JCSM-646-66 (TS), 6 Oct 66.

23. JCSM-645-66 (TS), 6 Oct 66; JCSM-646-66, 6 Oct 66.

Chapter V

1. Van Staaveren, 1966, ch V.

2. CM-1906-66 (TS), 8 Nov 66; memo (TS), Gravenstine to AFCHO, 22 Nov 67.

3. Memo (TS), SAF to SECDEF, 10 Nov 66, no subj, w/atch Interim Reply on Air Staff Action Items Resulting from SECDEF Trip to SEA, 10-14 Oct 66, in OSAF.

4. PACAF rprt (S), SEA Air Ops, Nov 66, pp 1-4; rprt (TS), An Eval of the Effects of the Air Campaign on NVN and Laos, Nov 66, both in Dir/Plans; Van Staaveren, 1966, pp 63-66.

5. PACAF rprts (S), SEA Air Ops, Nov 66, pp 1-9; Dec 66, pp 1-8, both in Dir/Plans.

6. Ibid.; Project CHECO SEA Rprt (TS), 15 Jul 67, subj: R/T, Jul 65-Dec 66, pp 98-99; Hist (TS), CINCPAC, 1966, vol II, pp 504-05 and 512; Balt Sun 18 Dec 66; N.Y. Times, 16 Dec 66.

7. Balt Sun, 14 Dec 66; N.Y. Times, 15 Dec 66; Wash Post, 15 and 16 Dec 66.

8. Project CHECO SEA Rprt (TS), 15 Jul 67, subj: R/T, Jul 65-Dec 66, pp 99-100.

9. Ibid.; N.Y. Times, 27 Dec 66.

10. Project CHECO SEA Rprt (TS), 25 May 67, subj: Air Interdiction in SEA, 1965-1966, p 68; PACAF rprt (S), SEA Air Ops, Nov 66, pp 1-9; Dec 66, pp 1-8.

11. Ibid.; app 1 and 2; N.Y. Times, 26, 27 Dec 66, and 3 Jan 67.

12. CASFM-D-25-66 (TS), 23 Nov 66; memo (TS), Brig Gen E.A. McDonald, Dep Dir of Plans for War Plans to Dir/Plans, 16 Dec 66, subj: Combat Beaver, both in Dir/Plans; Hist (S), Dir/Ops, Jul-Dec 66, pp 2-3 and 254.

13. Memo (TS), McDonald to Dir/Plans, 23 Nov 66; Hist (S), Dir/Ops, Jul-Dec 66, pp 2-3; Project CHECO SEA Rprt (TS), 15 Jul 67, subj: R/T, Jul 65-Dec 66, pp 94-95.

14. Project CHECO SEA Rprt (TS), 21 Jul 67, subj: Expansion of USAF Ops in SEA, 1966, p 111; PACAF rprts (S), SEA Air Ops, Nov 66, p 22; and Dec 66, p 25.

15. PACAF Chronology, Jul 65-Jun 66 (S), in AFCHO; PACAF rprts (S), SEA Air Ops, Nov 66, pp 1-9; Dec 66, pp 1-8; Project CHECO SEA Rprt (TS), 15 Jul 67, subj: R/T, Jul 65-Dec 66, p 118; USAF Mgt Summary (S), 6 Jan 67, p 70; Hist (TS), CINCPAC, 1966, vol II, pp 522-23; app 10 and 11.

16. Ltr (TS), CINCPAC to JCS, 22 Nov 66, subj: SA-Threat Conf Rpt, in Dir/Plans; Hist (TS), CINCPAC, 1966, vol II, pp 516-19.

Notes to Pages 66 - 71

17. Ltr (TS), CINCPAC to JCS, 22 Nov 66; JCS 2343/977 (TS), 16 Dec 66.

18. Memo (TS), Col E. T. Burnett, Dep Chief, Tac Div, Dir/Ops to Asst Dir of Plans for Jt and NSC Matters, 28 Nov 66, subj: Major Recommendations of the SA-2 Conf, in Dir/Plans; JCS 2343/977 (TS), 16 Dec 66; Hist (TS), CINCPAC, 1966, vol II, p 519.

19. Van Staaveren, 1966, pp 71-74.

20. Address (U), Gen McConnell before Jt Activities Briefing, Hq USAF, 23 Nov 66, in SAFOI; Testimony of McConnell on 9 May 66 before Senate Investigating Preparedness Subcmte (U), p 29; Van Staaveren, 1966, pp 71-74.

21. Address (U), Gen McConnell before the Houston, Texas Forum, 29 Nov 66, in SAFOI.

22. Project CHECO SEA Rprts (TS), 1 Mar 67, subj: Control of Air Strikes in SEA, pp 81-99; and 23 Oct 67, subj: The War in VN, pp 44-45; memo (TS), SAF to SECDEF, 3 Jun 67, subj: Possible Course of Action in SEA; memo (TS), SAF to SECDEF, 9 Jun 67, no subj, both in Dir/Plans; memo (TS), Echols to AFCHO, 27 Nov 67.

23. Hist (TS), CINCPAC, 1966, vol II, pp 510-12 and 606-07.

24. Address (U), Secy Brown before Aviation/Space Writers Assoc Mtg, Wash D.C., 8 Dec 66, in SAFOI; Balt Sun, 9 Dec 66; rprt (U), Selected Statements on VN by DOD and Other Admin Officials, 1 Jan-30 Jun 67, p 33, in SAFOI.

25. Testimony of Secy McNamara on 20 Feb 67 before House Subcmtes of the Cmte on Appns, 90th Cong, 1st Sess, Supplemental Def Appns for 1967. p 21; Van Staaveren, 1966 pp 48-50.

APPENDIX 4

U.S. Aircraft Losses in Southeast Asia[*]

Hostile Causes

1965

	North Vietnam	Laos	South Vietnam	Total
USAF	82	11	64	157
USN[+]	85	8	6	99
USMC[+]	3	3	0	6
TOTAL	170	22	70	262

1966

	North Vietnam	Laos	South Vietnam	Total
USAF	172	48	76	296
USN[+]	109	7	6	122
USMC[+]	4	5	14	33
TOTAL	285	60	96	451

Operational Causes

	1965	1966	Total
USAF	64	78	142
USN[+]	27	40	67
USMC[+]	10	12	22
TOTAL	101	130	231

---

* Excludes helicopters. Includes losses due to enemy mortar attacks.
+ USN and USMC figures subject to variations contingent on bookkeeping procedures.

SOURCE: Ops Review Gp, Dir/Ops, Hq USAF.

APPENDIX 5

USAF Combat Attrition in North Vietnam

1965*

Type of Sorties +	Sorties	Losses	Rate per 1,000 Sorties
Attack	11,599	63	5.43
CAP/Escort	5,675	7	1.23
Reconnaissance	3,294	9	2.73
Other	4,983	3	0.60
TOTAL	25,551	82	3.21

1966

Type of Sorties	Sorties	Losses	Rate per 1,000 Sorties
Attack	44,482	138	3.10
CAP/Escort	9,041	6	0.66
Reconnaissance	7,910	19	2.40
Other	16,587	9	0.54
TOTAL	78,020	172	2.20

* Bombing of North Vietnam began on 7 February 1965.
+ Excludes B-52 strikes.

SOURCE: Ops Review Gp, Dir/Ops, Hq USAF.

APPENDIX 6

U.S. Aircraft Losses to SA-2's

Date	Missiles Fired	Confirmed Losses			Probable Losses			Percent Confir'd	Effective Total
		USAF	USN	USMC	USAF	USN	USMC		
1965 *	180	5	5	0	0	1	0	5.6	6.1
1966	1,057	13	7	0	5	6	0	1.9	2.9
TOTAL	1,237	18	12	0	5	7	0	2.4	3.4

* The first SA-2 firings were sighted in July 1965.

SOURCE: Ops Review Gp, Dir/Ops, Hq USAF.

APPENDIX 7

SA-2 Sites in North Vietnam

	Jan	Mar	Jun*	Sep	Dec
1965	0	0	4	23	64
1966	64	100	115	144	151

* The first SA-2 site was detected in April 1965.

SOURCE: Ops Review Gp, Dir/Ops, Hq USAF.

APPENDIX 8

Light and Medium Antiaircraft Artillery Guns in North Vietnam

	Jan	Feb*	Mar	Jun	Sep	Dec
1965	--	1,156	1,418	1,643	2,636	2,551
1966	2,884	3,092	3,159	4,123	5,009	6,398

* Bombing of North Vietnam began on 7 February 1965.

SOURCE: Ops Review Gp, Dir/Ops, Hq USAF.

APPENDIX 9

U.S. Aircraft Losses in Aerial Combat

	USAF	USN	USMC	Total
1965	2*	0	0	2
1966	5+	4++	0	9
TOTAL	7	4	0	11

* Consisted of 2 F-105's.
+ Consisted of 3 F-105's, 1 F-4C, 1 RC-47 and two "probables", 1 F-4C and 1 A-1.
++ Consisted of 3 F8's and 1 KA3. No "probables."

SOURCE: Ops Review Gp, Dir/Ops, Hq USAF.

APPENDIX 10

North Vietnamese Aircraft Losses in Aerial Combat

	MIG-15's	MIG-17's	MIG-21's	Total*
Destroyed by:		1965		
USAF	0	2	0	2
USN	0	3	0	3
USMC	0	0	0	0
TOTAL	0	5	0	5
		1966		
USAF	0	12	5	17
USN	0	4	2	6
USMC	0	0	0	0
TOTAL	0	16	7	23

* No "probables" listed.

SOURCE: Ops Review Gp, Dir/Ops, Hq USAF.

GLOSSARY

AB	Air Base
A/C	Aircraft
AFCHO	USAF Historical Division Liaison Office
Aflds	Airfields
Appns	Appropriations
Asst CS/I	Assistant Chief of Staff, Intelligence
Atchd	Attached
CAP	Combat Air Patrol
CHECO	Contemporary Historical Evaluation of Counterinsurgency
CIA	Central Intelligence Agency
CINCPAC	Commander-in-Chief, Pacific
CM	Chairman's Memo
CMCM	Commandant Marine Corps Memo
CNO	Chief of Naval Operations
Comd	Command
COMUSMACV	Commander, U.S. Military Command, Vietnam
Conf	Conference
CSAFM	Chief of Staff Air Force Memo
CY	Calendar Year
DAF	Department of the Air Force
Dam	Damage
DCS/P&O	Deputy Chief of Staff, Plans and Operations
DCS/P&R	Deputy Chief of Staff, Programs and Resources
Dep	Deputy
Des	Destroyed
DIA	Defense Intelligence Agency
Dir	Director, Directorate
Dir/Ops	Directorate of Operations
Dir/Plans	Directorate of Plans
DMZ	Demilitarized Zone
DOD	Department of Defense
ECM	Electronic Countermeasure
Eval	Evaluation
FAC	Forward Air Controller
Ftr	Fighter
Gp	Group
Hist	History
ICC	International Control Commission
Intvw	Interview
JCS	Joint Chiefs of Staff
JCSM	Joint Chiefs of Staff Memo
Jt	Joint

(This page is Unclassified)

Lat	Latitude
LOC	Lines of Communication
Long	Longitude
MACV	Military Assistance Command
Mgt	Management
Mil	Military
NSC	National Security Council
NVN	North Vietnam
Ops	Operations
OSD	Office, Secretary of Defense
OSAF	Office, Secretary of the Air Force
Pac	Pacific
PACAF	Pacific Air Forces
POL	Petroleum Oil and Lubricants
Pres	President
Prog	Program
RP	Route Package
Rprt	Report
R/T	Rolling Thunder
Rqmts	Requirements
SA	Systems Analysis
SAC	Strategic Air Command
SAF	Secretary of the Air Force
SAFOI	Secretary of the Air Force Office of Information
SECDEF	Secretary of Defense
Secy	Secretary
SM	Secretary's Memo
SN	Secretary of the Navy
SOD	Secretary of Defense
Strat	Strategic
SVN	South Vietnam
Sys	Systems
Tac	Tactical
TFS	Tactical Fighter Squadron
USAFE	United States Air Force, Europe
VC	Viet Cong
VN	Vietnam
VNAF	Vietnamese Air Force

DISTRIBUTION

HQ USAF

1. SAF-OS
2. SAF-US
3. SAF-FM
4. SAF-RD
5. SAF-IL
6. SAF-GC
7. SAF-LL
8. SAF-OI
9. SAF-OIX
10. SAF-AAR
11. AFCSA
12. AFCSAMI
13. AFCVC
14. AFCVS
15. AFBSA
16. AFGOA
17. AFIIS
18. AFJAG
19. AFNIN
20. AFADS
21. AFAMA
22. AFOAP
23. AFOAPB
24. AFOAPD
25. AFOAPG
26. AFOCC
27. AFPMC
28. AFRDC
29. AFRDC-D
30. AFRDD
31. AFRDDH
32. AFRDQ
33. AFRDQR
34. AFRRP
35. AFSLP
36. AFSME
37. AFSMS
38. AFSPD
39. AFSSS
40. AFXDC
41. AFXDO
42. AFXOP
43. AFXOPA
44-45. AFXOPG
46-47. AFXOS
48. AFXOX
49. AFXPD
50. AFXPDW
51. AFXPDWC
52. AFXPDWF
53. AFXPDWW
54. AFXPDO
55. AFXPDIP
56. AFXPDP
57. AFXPDR

MAJOR COMMANDS

58. AAC
59. ADC
60. AFCS
61. AFLC
62. AFSC
63. CAC
64. MAC
65-67. PACAF
68-69. SAC
70-71. TAC
72. USAFSO
73. USAFSS

OTHER

74-75. RAND
76-78. ASI(ASHAF-A)
79-100. AFCHO (Stock)

AFCHO PUBLICATIONS

Below is a list of AFCHO historical monographs dealing with various aspects of the conflict in Southeast Asia which may be obtained on loan or for permanent retention. Copies may be obtained by calling Oxford 6-6565 or by forwarding a written request.

USAF Counterinsurgency Doctrines and Capabilities, 1961-1962. (S-Noforn)

USAF Special Air Warfare Doctrines and Capabilities, 1963. (S-Noforn)

USAF Plans and Policies in South Vietnam, 1961-1963. (TS-Noforn)

USAF Plans and Policies in South Vietnam and Laos, 1964. (TS-Noforn)

USAF Plans and Operations in Southeast Asia, 1965. (TS-Noforn)

USAF Logistic Plans and Policies in Southeast Asia, 1965. (TS-Noforn)

USAF Logistic Plans and Policies in Southeast Asia, 1965. (TS-Noforn)

USAF Deployment Planning For Southeast Asia, 1966. (TS-Noforn)

In addition to the above monographs, there are a large number of historical studies dealing with Vietnam operations prepared by Project CHECO and by the various participating and supporting commands, including organizational histories down to the wing and squadron level.

www.ingramcontent.com/pod-product-compliance
Lightning Source LLC
Chambersburg PA
CBHW080441170426
43195CB00017B/2844